D1550932

Chuck Yeager

Chuck Yeager

These and other titles are included in The Importance Of biography series:

Maya Angelou	Ernest Hemingway
Louis Armstrong	Adolf Hitler
James Baldwin	Thomas Jefferson
Lucille Ball	John F. Kennedy
The Beatles	Martin Luther King Jr.
Alexander Graham Bell	Bruce Lee
Napoleon Bonaparte	Lenin
Julius Caesar	John Lennon
Rachel Carson	Abraham Lincoln
Fidel Castro	Charles Lindbergh
Charlie Chaplin	Douglas MacArthur
Charlemagne	Margaret Mead
Winston Churchill	Golda Meir
Christopher Columbus	Mother Teresa
Leonardo da Vinci	Muhammad
James Dean	John Muir
Charles Dickens	Richard M. Nixon
Walt Disney	Georgia O'Keefe
Dr. Seuss	Pablo Picasso
F. Scott Fitzgerald	Edgar Allan Poe
Henry Ford	Queen Elizabeth I
Anne Frank	Franklin Roosevelt
Benjamin Franklin	Jonas Salk
Mohandas Gandhi	Margaret Sanger
John Glenn	William Shakespeare
Jane Goodall	Frank Sinatra
Martha Graham	Tecumseh
Lorraine Hansberry	Simon Wiesenthal

THE IMPORTANCE OF

Chuck Yeager

by Michael J. Martin

LUCENT
BOOKS®

THOMSON
━━━✦━━━ ™
GALE

San Diego • Detroit • New York • San Francisco • Cleveland • New Haven, Conn. • Waterville, Maine • London • Munich

LIBRARY OF CONGRESS CATALOGING-IN-PUBLICATION DATA

Martin, Michael J., 1948–
    Chuck Yeager / by Michael J. Martin.
       p. cm. — (Importance of)
Summary: Relates how the young pilot distinguished himself in World War II and
subsequently became the first person to break the sonic barrier.
Includes bibliographical references and index.
    ISBN 1-59018-284-7 (lib : alk. paper)
    1. Yeager, Chuck, 1923—Juvenile literature. 2. Air pilots—United States—Biography—
Juvenile literature. [1. Yeager, Chuck, 1923–. 2. Air pilots.] I. Title. II. Series.
    TL540 .Y4 M37 2004
    623.7'46048'092—dc21

                                               2002151714

Contents

Foreword

THE IMPORTANCE OF biography series deals with individuals who have made a unique contribution to history. The editors of the series have deliberately chosen to cast a wide net and include people from all fields of endeavor. Individuals from politics, music, art, literature, philosophy, science, sports, and religion are all represented. In addition, the editors did not restrict the series to individuals whose accomplishments have helped change the course of history. Of necessity, this criterion would have eliminated many whose contribution was great, though limited. Charles Darwin, for example, was responsible for radically altering the scientific view of the natural history of the world. His achievements continue to impact the study of science today. Others, such as Chief Joseph of the Nez Percé, played a pivotal role in the history of their own people. While Joseph's influence does not extend much beyond the Nez Percé, his nonviolent resistance to white expansion and his continuing role in protecting his tribe and his homeland remain an inspiration to all.

These biographies are more than factual chronicles. Each volume attempts to emphasize an individual's contributions both in his or her own time and for posterity. For example, the voyages of Christopher Columbus opened the way to European colonization of the New World. Unquestionably, his encounter with the New World brought monumental changes to both Europe and the Americas in his day. Today, however, the broader impact of Columbus's voyages is being critically scrutinized. *Christopher Columbus*, as well as every biography in The Importance Of series, includes and evaluates the most recent scholarship available on each subject.

Each author includes a wide variety of primary and secondary source quotations to document and substantiate his or her work. All quotes are footnoted to show readers exactly how and where biographers derive their information, as well as provide stepping stones to further research. These quotations enliven the text by giving readers eyewitness views of the life and times of each individual covered in The Importance Of series.

Finally, each volume is enhanced by photographs, bibliographies, chronologies, and comprehensive indexes. For both the casual reader and the student engaged in research, The Importance Of biographies will be a fascinating adventure into the lives of people who have helped shape humanity's past and present, and who will continue to shape its future.

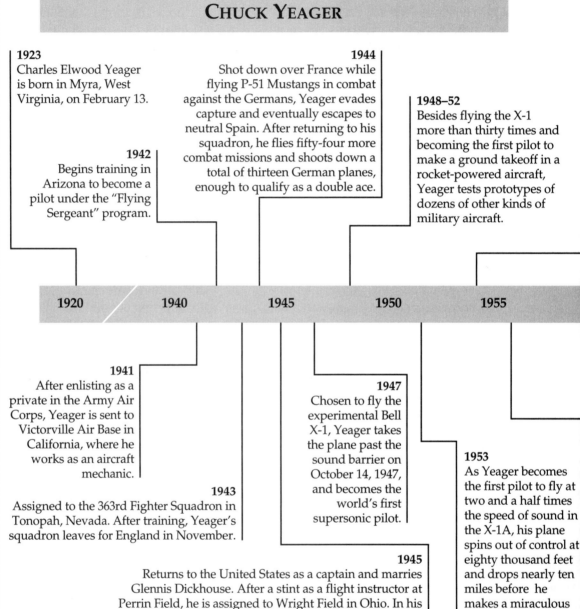

IMPORTANT DATES IN THE LIFE OF CHUCK YEAGER

1923
Charles Elwood Yeager is born in Myra, West Virginia, on February 13.

1942
Begins training in Arizona to become a pilot under the "Flying Sergeant" program.

1944
Shot down over France while flying P-51 Mustangs in combat against the Germans, Yeager evades capture and eventually escapes to neutral Spain. After returning to his squadron, he flies fifty-four more combat missions and shoots down a total of thirteen German planes, enough to qualify as a double ace.

1948–52
Besides flying the X-1 more than thirty times and becoming the first pilot to make a ground takeoff in a rocket-powered aircraft, Yeager tests prototypes of dozens of other kinds of military aircraft.

1920   **1940**   **1945**   **1950**   **1955**

1941
After enlisting as a private in the Army Air Corps, Yeager is sent to Victorville Air Base in California, where he works as an aircraft mechanic.

1943
Assigned to the 363rd Fighter Squadron in Tonopah, Nevada. After training, Yeager's squadron leaves for England in November.

1947
Chosen to fly the experimental Bell X-1, Yeager takes the plane past the sound barrier on October 14, 1947, and becomes the world's first supersonic pilot.

1953
As Yeager becomes the first pilot to fly at two and a half times the speed of sound in the X-1A, his plane spins out of control at eighty thousand feet and drops nearly ten miles before he makes a miraculous recovery and lands safely.

1945
Returns to the United States as a captain and marries Glennis Dickhouse. After a stint as a flight instructor at Perrin Field, he is assigned to Wright Field in Ohio. In his capacity as maintenance officer he flies the latest fighter planes and his skills catch the attention of superiors.

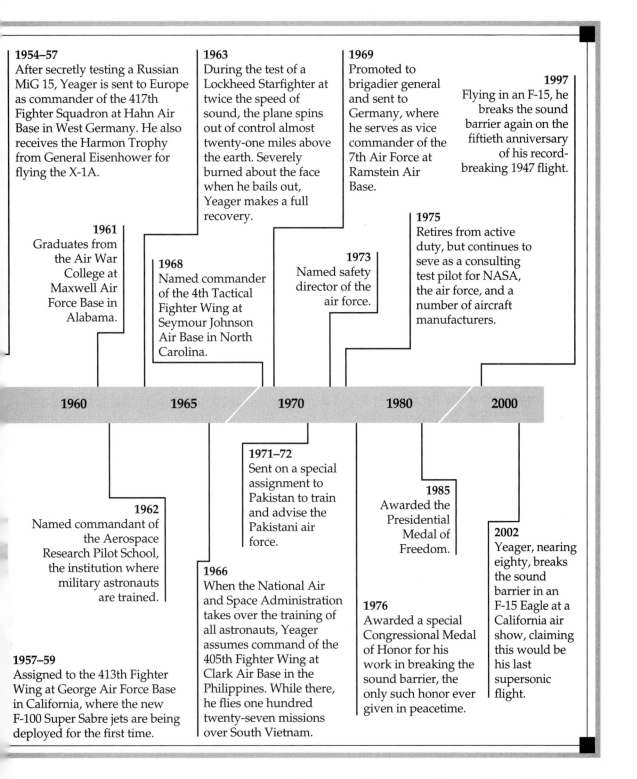

1954–57
After secretly testing a Russian MiG 15, Yeager is sent to Europe as commander of the 417th Fighter Squadron at Hahn Air Base in West Germany. He also receives the Harmon Trophy from General Eisenhower for flying the X-1A.

1963
During the test of a Lockheed Starfighter at twice the speed of sound, the plane spins out of control almost twenty-one miles above the earth. Severely burned about the face when he bails out, Yeager makes a full recovery.

1969
Promoted to brigadier general and sent to Germany, where he serves as vice commander of the 7th Air Force at Ramstein Air Base.

1997
Flying in an F-15, he breaks the sound barrier again on the fiftieth anniversary of his record-breaking 1947 flight.

1961
Graduates from the Air War College at Maxwell Air Force Base in Alabama.

1968
Named commander of the 4th Tactical Fighter Wing at Seymour Johnson Air Base in North Carolina.

1973
Named safety director of the air force.

1975
Retires from active duty, but continues to seve as a consulting test pilot for NASA, the air force, and a number of aircraft manufacturers.

1960   **1965**   **1970**   **1980**   **2000**

1962
Named commandant of the Aerospace Research Pilot School, the institution where military astronauts are trained.

1971–72
Sent on a special assignment to Pakistan to train and advise the Pakistani air force.

1985
Awarded the Presidential Medal of Freedom.

2002
Yeager, nearing eighty, breaks the sound barrier in an F-15 Eagle at a California air show, claiming this would be his last supersonic flight.

1966
When the National Air and Space Administration takes over the training of all astronauts, Yeager assumes command of the 405th Fighter Wing at Clark Air Base in the Philippines. While there, he flies one hundred twenty-seven missions over South Vietnam.

1976
Awarded a special Congressional Medal of Honor for his work in breaking the sound barrier, the only such honor ever given in peacetime.

1957–59
Assigned to the 413th Fighter Wing at George Air Force Base in California, where the new F-100 Super Sabre jets are being deployed for the first time.

A Supersonic Pioneer

One of the more memorable American heroes to come out of World War II was a determined young West Virginian named Chuck Yeager. A fighter pilot with exceptional eyesight and legendary flying skills, Yeager flew sixty-one combat missions over Europe. During his tour of duty he risked death countless times and shot down twelve enemy fighters while winning a Silver Star and a Distinguished Flying Cross.

But, unlike the achievements of almost all his peers, Yeager's death-defying exploits continued long after the war ended. His superb flying skills and rare ability to think clearly under pressure made him indispensable as aviation technology made the dangerous transition from propeller-driven to jet-propelled and rocket-propelled aircraft.

Chuck Yeager was at the forefront of that transition. Before him, no pilot had ever gone faster than the speed of sound. In fact, many experts believed that such a feat was physically impossible. In time, Yeager proved the experts wrong. Day after day he risked his life by climbing into rocket-powered experimental aircraft and blasting off into the unknown. Not only did he eventually break the so-called sound barrier, but he also flew to the very edge of space.

Once Yeager had shown the world that supersonic flight was possible, he was delighted to find that his skills were in more demand than ever. An entirely new air force was being created, and pilots with steely nerves and exceptional skill were needed to test the prototypes of dozens of different kinds of airplanes. These prototypes often had design flaws and nasty flying quirks that could only be discovered in the air. The test pilot's challenge was to discover any such "bugs" before they killed him.

It was extremely dangerous work that killed many good pilots, but Yeager's unique abilities allowed him to thrive in this high-pressure atmosphere. He flew the first versions of fighters, bombers, cargo planes, and dozens of other kinds of aircraft. In addition to his own test flights, Yeager was often called upon to fly alongside other pilots while they tested various kinds of experimental aircraft. This was called "flying chase," and a test pilot in trouble would often call on the help of a chase pilot. The description of one close call serves to demonstrate why Yeager was considered the best in the business.

A MASTER AT WORK

In the summer of 1951 test pilot Carl Bellinger was just lifting off the runway from a base in the Mojave Desert in a rocket-propelled experimental fighter called the X-F 91. On this particular morning Yeager had been assigned to fly chase. With a typically masterful piece of flying he positioned his plane so that it was flying right beside the X-F 91 just as it left the ground. His proximity and keen eyesight saved Bellinger precious seconds when they mattered most.

Chuck Yeager (pictured here when he was a colonel) was the first pilot to break the sound barrier. For this and other achievements, Yeager is considered a pioneer of aviation.

"Old buddy," said Yeager over the radio, "I hate to tell you, but a piece of molten engine just shot out your exhaust, and you'd better do something quick." Yeager meant that Bellinger should dump his fuel tanks and land as quickly as possible. With typical humor, he added, "Don't you hit my house with those tanks, either!"[1]

The joke eased the tension of a desperate situation. At only five hundred feet above the desert floor, Bellinger was too low to eject from the plane; his parachute would never open in time to save him. Meanwhile, Bellinger could feel the heat of the fire behind him as the cockpit filled with dense, black smoke at an alarming rate. Trying to keep the panic out of his voice, he radioed Yeager and told him that the smoke was blinding him.

Calmly, as if he were giving directions to the nearest grocery store, Yeager replied, "Do a two-seventy to the right and keep it tight."[2] Although unable to see, Bellinger followed Yeager's clear, concise instructions and soon had his plane lined up for a landing. When he touched down Yeager was right beside him. The second Bellinger's plane rolled to a stop, he opened his canopy and dived out. By the time he had climbed up on Yeager's wing, his own plane's tail had already melted off. When the fire trucks arrived a few moments later the X-F 91 was burnt to ashes. The two pilots taxied away from the scene with Yeager laughing and shaking his head over yet another narrow escape.

Although Yeager never lost a pilot while flying chase, he had many such close calls. Yet, in the same way that he guided pilots like Bellinger to a safe landing, he helped aviation into the supersonic age. But Yeager's service to his country did not end there. He flew to the edge of space, then helped train the men who would one day become astronauts and space shuttle pilots. Although he will always be best known as the man who broke the sound barrier, his contributions go far beyond that achievement. Despite incredible danger, Chuck Yeager was always pushing ahead into the unknown. He richly deserves his reputation as one of aviation's true pioneers.

Chapter

1 The Hillbilly from Hamlin

Chuck Yeager grew up in one of the poorest, most isolated counties in America. Born near Hamlin, West Virginia, on February 13, 1923, he was not even seven years old when the Great Depression began. Perhaps in response to the economic hardships of his early years, he grew up to be an unusually hardworking and self-reliant young man. The self-sufficiency he learned in the hills around Hamlin served him well for the rest of his life.

The second of five children born to Albert and Susie Mae Yeager, Charles Elwood "Chuck" Yeager had only to look at his parents to know the value of hard work. Like many men during the 1920s and 1930s, Albert Yeager supported his family by taking any available job that came his way. One of Chuck's most vivid early memories was the time his dad came home with his face and hands heavily bandaged. He had been burned from a flash fire that had exploded as he shoveled coal into a locomotive's firebox.

Until then Chuck had not realized how tough his father's life was. His dad never complained, but during most of Chuck's childhood he was away from home at least six days a week, working either for the railroad or in the gas fields of West Vir-

ginia. Meanwhile, Chuck's mother, a nononsense woman, labored from dawn to dusk, cooking, cleaning, canning, and gardening. She was most responsible for raising Chuck, his older brother Roy, and his younger brother Hal, Jr.

AN AWFUL ACCIDENT

Chuck's siblings included two younger sisters, Pansy Lee and Doris Ann, but Doris Ann died as a toddler when a shotgun accidentally discharged. As an adult Chuck Yeager recalled that his parents were so devastated by the loss of their little girl that they refused to speak of the accident ever again:

> Even when my older brother, Roy, at the age of six, accidentally shot and killed our little sister, Doris, Mom buried her feelings—so deeply that when Glennis [Yeager's wife] asked her about the tragedy years later, she didn't want to talk about it, and never did. Dad didn't vent his grief over Doris' death either, at least directly. Instead, he grabbed Roy and me soon after it happened and gave us some intensive lessons in how to handle

firearms safely. I guess he felt he had to make something constructive out of the loss, which he did.[3]

Though Chuck was only four and a half at the time, the incident seems to have made a strong impression on him. His realization that life can end so quickly perhaps explains

A railroad worker waves from the side of a boxcar. Yeager's father supported the family by working for the railroad sometimes.

his lifelong habit of making the most of every day and his aversion to spending time on anything that does not interest him.

AN EXPLORER IN OVERALLS

From the very beginning he loved to explore. "As a barefoot kid in bib overalls," Chuck recalled years later, "I used to wander the West Virginia woods for countless hours, always wanting to see what was around the next bend."[4] While wandering the rugged hills he usually carried a gun. Just about every kid in Hamlin knew how to hunt, and Chuck's skills quickly made him one of the town's best marksmen. With his 20/10 vision he could fire a .22 rifle accurately by the age of six. Often he would rise before dawn and go off hunting by himself before school. If his hunt had been successful he would clean his squirrels or rabbits, leave the small game on the front porch, and then head off to class, pleased to have provided a little extra food for that day's dinner table.

Whenever Chuck was doing something that interested him he tended to concentrate completely on the task. His ability to do so would work to his advantage later in life, but it got him in trouble as a kid. More than once he became so engrossed in hunting that he was late for school. (Coincidentally, the word *yeager* means hunter in German.) Although Chuck spent most of his free time hunting and exploring in the hills, he also fished for suckers and bass in the nearby Mud River. He notes his grandfather's considerable influence on him around this time:

> It was Grandpa Yeager who taught me so much about how the natural world works, how to hunt and fish and find shelter, that I could have survived, in style, alone in the woods, from the age of eight onward. . . . You just *had* to live off the land if you lived around Hamlin because money was in such ridiculously short supply.[5]

By the time Chuck was eight, the family had moved into a bigger house in Hamlin that included a large plot of land. Besides growing their own vegetables in a big garden, the family raised chickens and hogs and kept a cow to provide milk and butter. The move—plus the fact that their father was away from home from Sunday until Friday night—meant that Chuck and Roy had plenty of chores, both before and after school.

In addition to helping out in the garden, the boys slopped the hogs and milked the cow twice a day. In summer they made extra money by picking blackberries to sell at ten cents a gallon. Other "crops" they harvested included wild grapes, hickory nuts, black walnuts, persimmons, and the edible fruits of the paw-paw tree.

A Craving for Action

Looking back on his childhood more than fifty years later, Yeager can barely remember

---

A Curious Kid

Many years after his air force career ended Chuck Yeager retired to the foothills of the Sierra Nevada mountains in California. In explaining his attraction to those moutains in the book, Press On!, *Yeager hinted at the kind of restless kid he had been back in West Virginia.*

"As a barefoot kid in bib overalls . . . my feet were so callused they were tougher than any shoes. I don't think I was looking for anything in particular on those day-long jaunts; I was just an incredibly curious kid with a vague notion that one of these days I'd discover some grand, new wonder, maybe a place that would be some kind of Shangri-La, where the trees and rocks and the water formed a scene more beautiful than anyplace else on earth. It was a childish fantasy and I eventually forgot about it—until the day, very much later, after I'd returned from the war and was living far from the fields and mountains of my home state, when I finally found that special place that I'd been searching for."

a moment when he did not have something to do. That was just as well since he was the kind of kid who craved action. Sitting in a classroom was sheer torture, and he could not wait for weekends and vacations. Chuck's restless spirit was also evident in his competitive nature. Whether swinging like Tarzan on the vines that hung over the local swimming hole or racing down a snow-covered hill on homemade skis or bobsleds, he always tried to be the best.

Although Chuck had little true leisure time, he did find a number of ways to get into trouble, even in the woods. Once, he and Roy watched in secret as a moonshiner hid jugs of illegal alcohol in a hollow log. When he left the area they stole his jugs and sold them in town for a quarter a gallon. But they were so scared of what might happen if he found out that they never did it again.

Another slightly less dangerous form of thievery involved late-summer swims up-river to fields where watermelon grew. Chuck and his friends would quietly roll the melons into the river and then float down-

Children speed down a snow-covered hill on their sleds. Yeager was competitive in every activity, even sledding.

He Finished What He Started

Chuck Yeager believed the lessons he learned in his dad's garage carried over to the rest of his life. In his book, Press On!, *he explained why—and how he and his brother communicated with their dad through the family car.*

"There weren't too many bigger responsibilities in the Yeager household than that old Chevy. If the family car broke down, that meant a lot of money—money that we didn't always have. So we put in the gas for him, checked the water and oil, and hit all of the many lube points you had to keep greased in those days. We learned about engines and we also learned about seeing a job through to the end too. That in itself is a valuable lesson. Much later in life, at Edwards [Air Force Base], I noticed that my ability to push through to the end of the task was a big difference between me and the other test pilots. If the job was, say, to take the X1-A out to 2.5 Mach, and it started going haywire about 2.3, most other guys would back off. . . . I had the discipline to keep going, to finish what I'd been told to do despite any distractions. Partly this was due to my combat experience, which is something most other test pilots didn't have. But the idea of finishing what I started was really ingrained in me much earlier, in the family garage . . . .

That old car, in a way, was like a blank slate on which we said the things that, being Yeagers, we weren't about to say to each other outright. When Dad turned it over to us for servicing, the message was, 'It's an important job, but I know you can handle it.' When we gave it back, we were saying, 'Thanks, we've done our best for you.' It was communication. It was trust. It was respect. In any language, that adds up to a lot."

stream with them until they found a secluded place to eat where they did not have to worry about an angry farmer unexpectedly showing up with a shotgun loaded with rock salt.

Fascinated by Speed and Machines

Yeager recalls a narrow escape from injury during another boyhood adventure:

O'ER THE RAMPARTS WE WATCH

UNITED STATES
ARMY AIR FORCES

Army Air Force recruitment posters like this one enticed many young American men to enlist. Yeager joined the army in order to see the world.

When I was nearly thirteen, I climbed into a '33 Dodge truck belonging to our neighbor, Mr. Sites. Dad let us fool around with his truck, and I thought I knew how to drive it. I decided to drive Mr. Sites's truck off our hill. I kicked it out of gear and took off, going fifty-five with no brakes on. I tried, but failed, to get into low gear and barely turned the corner at the bottom of the hill, where there was a vacant lot loaded with empty asphalt drums from recent road paving. I hit those drums with a crash that was heard for miles. Man, I got out of there using my own two feet.[6]

It was not surprising that Chuck was fascinated by cars and trucks. He had inherited his father's superior mechanical abilities. An expert self-taught mechanic, Albert Yeager spent a lot of time tinkering with motors, generators, or the engine in his Chevy truck. While he worked, Chuck and Roy watched and helped. Chuck learned quickly. Before long he could take a motor apart and put it back together without help. Years later his uncanny ability to quickly understand how complicated machinery worked would amaze college-educated professional engineers.

A Teen with Not Enough Time

Chuck's mechanical abilities were apparent by the time he reached high school, but he also showed a natural aptitude for mathematics—his geometry teacher considered him her best student. Always a quick study, he was most interested in subjects that had practical applications. He earned his best grades in typing and math, but thought English and history had little to do with his life, and his grades in those subjects suffered accordingly.

By the time he entered high school, Chuck's days were full: Besides chores, homework, and hunting and fishing, he had found a job sweeping out the local pool hall for ten dollars a month. He had also discovered the opposite sex. With other high school friends, he hung around

Hamlin's recreation center, flirting with girls, listening to records, and playing ping-pong.

By Chuck's senior year it seemed there were simply too few hours in the day to do all the things he wanted to do. He began staying out late at night, playing pool or poker with friends, and chasing girls. That kind of behavior got him in hot water with his mother. Upset with his habits, she began locking the door when he stayed out too late. Chuck got around that by climbing a tree and sneaking into the house through an upstairs bedroom window.

His exasperated mother was perhaps relieved by the decision Chuck made in the summer of 1941. By then he had his high school diploma, but going on to college was never really an option—the family could not afford college tuition, and in any case, Chuck had never thought of himself as much of a scholar. So when an Army Air Corps recruiter came through town it was not hard to talk Chuck into enlisting for a couple of years. He figured that being in the military would allow him to see some of the rest of the world, and it might even be fun. He had no idea then that the Army Air Corps would evolve into the air force—or that he had taken the first step on a journey that would one day make him the best-known pilot in the world.

2 A Hunter Takes Wing

Eighteen-year-old Chuck Yeager entered the military with the right qualifications at the right time. As he would soon discover, he possessed the exact skills and temperament necessary to become a top-notch fighter pilot, and the armed forces would soon need expert pilots as never before. However, a desire to fly was not why he joined the Army Air Corps. "I had no knowledge of airplanes and I couldn't have cared less about them,"[7] he would later recall.

Growing up in isolated Hamlin, the only plane he had ever seen up close was a small Beechcraft that had crash-landed in a nearby cornfield. Despite his lack of exposure to airplanes, however, his experiences in Hamlin proved the perfect preparation for an adventurous life in the air. His mechanical aptitude, acute eyesight, hunting ability, and competitiveness, plus the kind of hand-eye coordination necessary to become an expert marksman, were priceless assets for a fighter pilot.

Unlike many of the men who would go on to become pilots during World War II, Yeager had not dreamed of flying all his life. He had not hung around airports, watching planes or begging for rides. Not until he joined the service and became an airplane mechanic did his ambition to become a pilot develop. Even then, he did not immediately realize that he would be an excellent fighter pilot candidate.

His timing, however, was perfect. In December 1941, only a few months after he enlisted as a private in the Army Air Corps, the Japanese bombed Pearl Harbor and plunged the United States into World War II. In the months immediately after the attack there was a rush to build thousands of new planes and train the pilots to fly them.

At first, though, it seemed that there was little likelihood that Chuck Yeager would become one of those pilots. Not long after the Japanese attack on Pearl Harbor, he was working as an aircraft mechanic at a base in Victorville, California. His first airplane ride there had not gone well. "I took my first ride in an [Beech] AT-11 that I was crew chief on at Victorville," he recalled years later. "I was deathly sick and puked all over the airplane, and I said to myself after the flight, 'You've made a big mistake.'"[8]

NO MORE KITCHEN PATROL

But then he heard about the "Flying Sergeant" program, without which he might

Smoke billows from the bombed deck of the USS West Virginia *in Pearl Harbor in 1941. World War II created an opportunity for Yeager to learn how to fly.*

have remained a mechanic for the duration of the war. Until then, military flight school was restricted to men qualified to become officers. That meant that almost all potential pilots were college-educated. Yet, because of the shortage of pilots, for a few months the Flying Sergeant program offered enlisted men like Yeager the rare opportunity to become pilots.

Despite his early brush with airsickness, Yeager's competitive nature asserted itself. He wanted to prove he was just as good as those "college boys." He also liked the idea

that pilots were paid $150 a month (compared with the $30 a month he was earning at the time). Besides, it seemed like a great way to get out of pulling K.P. (kitchen patrol) and guard duty, assignments he hated.

So he applied for the program and was selected in July 1942 and ordered to Luke Field, Arizona, for training. At first he wondered whether he would be able to keep up with colleagues who were older (he was only nineteen) and better educated. His rustic speech was also a source of discomfort. Until he left Hamlin, Yeager thought that everybody said "hit" when they meant "it" or "paper poke" when they meant "paper sack." Now people were laughing at the way he spoke and calling him a hillbilly.

Although self-conscious about his background, Yeager soon realized he had a gift for flying. After the first few test flights his stomach stopped fluttering and he actually began to enjoy the experience. Good pilots must operate a number of different controls simultaneously, and his fine sense of coordination allowed him to develop that skill faster than his classmates. His proficiency

A pilot prepares to land on the USS Hornet during World War II. During the war, the United States needed more pilots and recruited enlisted men like Yeager for flight school.

An Inauspicious Beginning

Bryan Ethier discussed Chuck Yeager's mechanical background (and how his flying career got off to a rather rocky start!) in an article for American History *published in the fall of 1997.*

"If Yeager was not predestined to fly the X-1, he was at least predisposed to enjoying a successful career as a test pilot. Born on February 13, 1923, Charles 'Chuck' Yeager developed a fondness for working with drilling equipment generators as a youngster growing up in Hamlin, West Virginia. His background served him well when he enlisted in the U.S. Army Air Corps in 1941, earning his pay as an airplane mechanic with the 363rd Squadron, then stationed in Nevada. Fixing motors was one thing, dealing with the queasiness of flight was another matter. On his first airplane ride, Yeager became miserably airsick."

earned him promotions, from private first class to corporal to flight officer.

A Gift for Flying

One instructor, impressed by how smoothly Yeager handled the controls after only fifteen hours of flying, commented that he must have done a considerable amount of flying as a civilian and was astounded to learn that that was not the case. Yeager loved the challenge of flight school and the fact that there was no way to fake being a good pilot. Once a pilot was in the air, how he talked or how many college courses he had taken were unimportant—all that mattered was how he flew. Before long Yeager was doing spins and dives and staging mock dogfights (aerial battles) with other pilots, which he almost always won. Moreover,

with his superior eyesight, he could see air or ground targets before anyone else in his group. When training was finished, Yeager received not only his pilot's wings but also his instructors' recommendation for fighter pilot school.

Yeager was thrilled, but the young daredevil was also relieved because he had expected to be thrown out of flight school for an incident that had occurred during his first months in the military. Bored while on guard duty in the Arizona desert one night, he had shown a fellow guard how to fire a .30-caliber machine gun by shooting short bursts out into the desert. Unfortunately, a stray bullet hit a rancher's horse. When the angry rancher demanded that the Army Air Corps pay for his dead horse, Yeager was court-martialed.

Fortunately, because of the wartime rush to train and enlist millions of men, Yeager's records did not catch up with him until after he had graduated as an enlisted flight officer in March 1943. Soon he was assigned to the 363rd Fighter Squadron at Tonopah, Nevada, and discovered that he loved the life of a fighter pilot:

> Those six months of squadron training were the happiest that I've ever been. Now that I was a fighter pilot, I couldn't imagine being anything else. We were hell-raising fighter jocks with plenty of swagger. When we weren't flying, we zipped on our leather flight jackets that told the world who we were and crowded into [Bud] Anderson's 1939 Ford convertible . . . and drove into Tonopah, a wide-open mining town.[9]

DEATH, A CONSTANT COMPANION

Playing hard—drinking, gambling, and all-around hell raising—was a release Yeager and his buddies needed to function and to forget. Fighter pilot training was extremely dangerous; thirteen of Yeager's fellow pilots were killed before they even made it into combat. Meanwhile, Yeager not only survived but excelled. Perhaps because of his mechanical aptitude he seemed to have a natural feel for what his first fighter plane—the P-39 Bell Airacobra—could do. The single-engine P-39 was a tricky airplane to fly and had a dangerous tendency to spin out of control after a stall. Although Yeager liked to push his plane to the limit, he seemed to know just what that limit was, unlike so many other young pilots.

Yeager's roommate and closest friend during this time was a Texan named Chuck McKee. On weekends Yeager and McKee would race jeeps out into the desert and hunt rabbits with Springfield rifles. During one of their hunting trips the pair befriended a local rancher, Joe Clifford, and his wife, who "adopted" the pilots in Yeager's squadron and often invited as many as fifteen at a time to stop by for dinner.

During practice flights Yeager and other pilots would fly low over the Clifford ranch. If Joe came outside waving a bed sheet, it meant that everyone was invited to come over for dinner that night. They must have been an unruly but entertaining bunch: The day after Joe mentioned that he would like to get rid of a tree that stood near the house, Yeager buzzed the tree and removed its top with the left wingtip of his P-39. For that stunt he was grounded from flying P-39s for a week, but he simply took off in another model and buzzed the Clifford ranch while most of the rest of his squadron was gathered around the table. By this time he had a well-deserved reputation as a "crazy hillbilly" who would try just about anything.

THIS PILOT STOOD OUT

In June 1943, Yeager's squadron was transferred to Santa Rosa, California, where the 363rd was to practice bomber escort and coastal patrol operations. Yeager, however, did not join his fellow pilots right away. Instead, he was ordered to Wright Field in Ohio to do some temporary test pilot duty. A new propeller had been designed for the P-39 and officials

Yeager's experience as a flight mechanic and his excellent piloting skills earned him an assignment testing a plane with a newly designed propeller.

were eager to see how it performed. Yeager was chosen because of his maintenance background and because he was such a fine pilot.

It was an easy assignment. All he had to do was fly the plane as frequently as possible while keeping records of its performance. As it happened, Hamlin was only about 130 miles away from Wright, and the temptation to fly home was impossible to resist. Ever curious about other kinds of planes, Yeager spent his spare time learning how to fly the P-47 fighter. One morning he took off in a P-47 and headed south. It was about seven in the morning when Yeager roared down Hamlin's Main Street at 500 miles per hour before pulling up and doing a series of rolls.

That evening, when he called home from Wright Field, he learned that he had caused quite an uproar. Farmers claimed that he had scared their animals and blown down their crops. One man insisted Yeager had flown under his pasture fence, and a woman was reportedly so frightened that she had to be taken to a hospital. Of course, the uproar did not stop Yeager from buzzing Hamlin again. Everyone knew who it was—he was Hamlin's only fighter pilot—and the town eventually got used to his impromptu air shows.

A California Girl

Later that summer Yeager returned to his squadron in California just in time to join his colleagues in a transfer to Oroville, a rugged area north of Sacramento, for the next stage of their training. On the first day there Yeager and a friend walked over to the local gymnasium to see if they could arrange a USO (United Service Organization) dance so the men in the squadron could meet some of the local girls. The social director for the town's USO was an attractive eighteen-year-old named Glennis Dickhouse.

Yeager asked her if she could organize a dance for that evening and got a sarcastic reply. "You expect me to whip up a

STRENGTH AND DETERMINATION

Glennis Dickhouse met her future husband when the squadron was transferred to Oroville, California. In Yeager: An Autobiography *she recalled the character she sensed underneath the surface of the young, unpolished West Virginian.*

"I really don't know why Chuck appealed to me so much, but obviously he did. He was very skinny in those days, although my girlfriends thought he was cute. At first he was unsure of himself around me, quite shy and a little intimidated. And his grammar was just atrocious; with his West Virginia accent, I barely understood every third word he spoke. Of course, I was very young, and those were dramatic times—all those young men preparing to go off to war. I had dated a few soldiers, but never a fighter pilot. I think that really impressed me, even if he was the most junior officer in his squadron. But, also, I sensed that he was a very strong and determined person, a poor boy who had started with nothing and would show the world what he was really made of. That was the kind of man I hoped one day to marry."

dance and find thirty girls on three hours' notice?" she asked. "No, you'll only need to come up with twenty-nine, because I want to take you,"[10] was Yeager's typically brash reply. Glennis did manage to find enough women for a dance that evening, and she even let herself be talked into going with Chuck. They danced a little and talked a lot—although she had trouble understanding his West Virginia accent. Chuck learned that they had much in common; she had grown up on a small ranch and, like Chuck, had learned to hunt, shoot, and fish as a youngster.

Glennis Dickhouse was an exceptionally self-reliant young woman. When her parents had moved to Oakland after her father found work at the shipyards there, she had stayed in Oroville on her own to finish high school. When Yeager met her, she had three jobs: secretary to the superintendent of schools, bookkeeper for a drugstore, and social director for the USO.

Yeager was impressed. She was pretty and talented and, although barely out of high school, was making more money than he was. During the two months he was at Oroville, Chuck and Glennis saw each other as much as possible. When Chuck left Oroville, Glennis gave him her picture and they promised to write each other. But with the entire world at war, it did not seem wise to make long-range plans.

A West Virginia Wild Man

From Oroville, Yeager's squadron went to Casper, Wyoming, in the fall of 1943 for the final stage of their training. Although he missed Glennis, Chuck was glad to get away from Oroville because he was in hot water again: He had flown to a nearby base and started some unauthorized dogfights with cadets in training there, provoking the outraged base commander to call Yeager a menace to safety.

Their training in Wyoming complete by early November, the squadron had one last big party scheduled before they departed for Europe and the war. Since there were plenty of antelope in the area (because of the war, they were not being hunted) Yeager figured that antelope steaks and roasts would be the perfect fare. After positioning a number of enlisted men near a road, he neatly herded a group of antelope toward them. Then he charged one of his guns to fire one shot at a time and laid about ten antelope right at the men's feet.

Before Yeager could enjoy the antelope steaks he had shot for the party, he had a near-fatal accident. On October 23, while participating in a practice attack on a bomber formation, his plane exploded at four hundred miles per hour. Yeager bailed out but was knocked unconscious when his chute opened. Discovered by a sheepherder, he was taken back to the base where doctors determined that he had fractured his back.

The injury was doubly painful for Yeager because it forced him to cancel a get-together he and Glennis had scheduled for that weekend and to lie incapacitated in a hospital bed instead. Somehow, by the time the squadron threw its big farewell bash at a hotel in downtown Casper, he was recovered enough to attend. Since it was his last weekend in the States, Glennis came up from California to say good-bye.

Yeager poses next to the nose of his fighter plane, Glamorous Glennis, *named after the woman he wanted to marry.*

Yeager's squadron climbed aboard a troop train bound for the East Coast on November 9. They would board the *Queen Mary* in New York and sail to England later that month, but as squadron maintenance officer, Yeager had to stay on a few extra days to pack and move equipment. On the day he left Wyoming for good, he called Glennis for a farewell conversation. By then he was certain she was the girl he wanted

to marry, but the future seemed too uncertain to tell her that just yet. They would continue to write each other, and once he reached England he even sent Glennis his paychecks to hold for him. He also told her that he had named his hot new fighter plane after her. Soon, a P-51 Mustang named *Glamorous Glennis* would be hunting the enemy in the skies over German-held Europe.

Chapter

3 Downed but Not Out: Behind Enemy Lines

Chuck Yeager's adventures during the first half of 1944 were filled with enough excitement and narrow escapes to last most men a lifetime. In Yeager's case they were just a preliminary for the rest of the war and for the kinds of danger he continued to face long after the fighting had ended. His unlikely survival only increased his confidence that, no matter how tough his situation, he would find a way out.

Ironically, Yeager's involvement in the air war almost ended barely three weeks after it began. His fighter squadron arrived in England on November 30, 1943, and was quickly assigned to a small airfield just off the North Sea coast some sixty miles northeast of London. Leiston Air Base was little more than three concrete runways surrounded by a sea of mud. Meanwhile, gales blowing off the North Sea made it chilly and uncomfortable, and the makeshift huts where the pilots spent most of their spare time were poorly heated. Just as in Wyoming the men found themselves huddling around stoves to keep warm.

It took several months of preparation before the squadron was ready to fly every day. Much of that preparation involved the pilots familiarizing themselves with a new plane. On December 19 the squadron received its first P-51 Mustangs, the best fighter planes in the Allied arsenal. With their supercharged Rolls Royce–designed engines and two-thousand-mile range, Mustangs were fast, powerful, and maneuverable. Although these one-seater fighter planes were tricky to fly, Yeager and his fellow pilots quickly fell in love with them. The new P-51s soon proved a worthy opponent for Germany's principal fighters, the Messerschmitt 109 and the Focke-Wulf 190. A later version of the 190, introduced in 1944, was faster and more maneuverable than the 109, but neither plane was as nimble in the air as the Mustang.

FLYING OVER ENEMY TERRITORY

Yeager's first mission was on February 11, 1944, only two days before his twenty-first birthday. It was just a routine patrol for enemy planes along the coast of occupied France. Still, like the other young pilots who were flying in a combat situation for the first time, Yeager remembers being scared to death. They encountered no enemy aircraft, but for the first time they heard the unsettling drone of German radar on their radios as antiaircraft gunners tried to lock on to

During the war, Allied planes flew in staggered formations like this to protect themselves from a German attack from behind.

their planes and the even more unsettling sound of antiaircraft shells exploding nearby.

"We called it flak," recalled Yeager's fellow pilot and good friend, Bud Anderson, "and it sometimes got so bad, to employ the cliché of the day, you could get out and walk on it."[11] The deeper into Germany a mission went, the heavier the flak. Yet the biggest threat came from enemy fighters. Allied pilots soon learned to ignore the flak

while their eyes swept the skies for approaching enemy fighters, remaining especially alert to ambush from the rear, a pilot's natural blind spot.

"The German who gets you is the one you'll never see,"[12] was a phrase pilots like Yeager heard over and over again. For maximum safety, fighter planes usually flew in staggered groups (or flights) of four planes. It was the job of each man to protect the rear of the plane slightly ahead of him. Unfortunately the pilot on the end—nick-named the "tail-end Charlie"—was in the most vulnerable position. He had no help in scanning the skies to his rear.

THE FIRST KILL

Most of Yeager's missions involved escort-ing heavy bombers deep into German terri-tory. In early March he saw his first real combat action in a daylight raid over Berlin:

> The Germans sent the 109s up and we tangled with them. I shot down my first airplane that day, a 109. First I overshot the guy 'cause I was doing everything wide open, and he was not as fast as I thought. I overshot and pulled up to do a big roll, then came in under him. It was just like in the films,

Parachutists prepare to make a landing. When Yeager was forced to parachute while flying a mission over Nazi-occupied France in 1944, he worried about gunfire from the ground.

you know, the pieces just fly off and they explode, and you just make damn sure none of the pieces hit you.[13]

It was Yeager's first kill—and would nearly be his last. The next day, March 5, 1944, he was flying his eighth mission as a tail-end Charlie in a group of fighters over southern France when a German Focke-Wulf 190 he never saw jumped him from behind. Without warning his cockpit seemed to explode as the German fighter's twenty-millimeter cannons began ripping his P-51 apart. In an instant his plane spun out of control, its engine on fire and a big hole in one wing.

As the P-51 began tumbling, Yeager was thrown free of his plane. (Fortunately he had just unfastened his seatbelt and the cockpit's canopy had already been shot away.) Even in this desperate situation—flat on his back and spinning wildly as he fell from sixteen thousand feet—Yeager was thinking clearly.

He knew that if he opened his parachute German fighters would try to strafe and kill him. Even if they somehow managed to miss shooting him, German soldiers on the ground would be waiting for him if he opened his chute early. They, too, might shoot him as he dangled helplessly from his parachute. Even if he were lucky, they would certainly capture him when he hit the ground. For any chance of survival and escape he would have to delay pulling his ripcord until the last possible moment. After plummeting more than two miles and with the ground coming up fast, Yeager pulled the ring that opened his parachute. By pulling on the shroud lines of his parachute he steered himself toward a forested

area where he landed in the top branches of a small pine tree. With repeated bouncing on the flexible sapling, Yeager was able to lower himself far enough so that he could safely jump to the ground.

ON THE RUN

Quickly folding up his parachute, he limped deeper into the woods, blood dripping from shrapnel wounds in his feet, hands, and right leg. Meanwhile, he could hear soldiers shouting in German and the rumble of vehicles as they searched for him. When he found a clump of thick underbrush, he decided to hide there at least until dark. Several times during the afternoon he heard low-flying planes overhead as the Germans continued their search.

Despite his wounds, Yeager was confident that he could survive in open country if he could just avoid the Germans. After all, he knew how to trap and hunt and live off the land, and he could always raid nearby farm fields for turnips and potatoes if necessary.

Every fighter pilot had a silk map of Europe sewn into his flight suit. Yeager pulled his out and begin studying it, trying to figure out the best way to cross the Pyrenees mountain range into Spain, a country that was neutral in the war. He estimated that he was about two hundred miles north of the border. By the time he reached it the mountain snows might have melted enough so that he could attempt a crossing.

His first concern, however, was avoiding capture. Toward dark it began to rain and he spent a cold, miserable night huddled

"I Didn't Have Much Hope"

When wartime letters from England to Glennis stopped arriving, she grew concerned. In time, as she explained in Yeager: An Autobiography, *Yeager's mother would contact her with disheartening news.*

"Chuck wrote regularly from England a couple of times a week. There were long delays getting his squadron combat-ready and he was frustrated. But after three months or so, he began seeing action. I had one letter in which he said they had finally flown over the Channel on a routine sweep to get combat experience, but then his letters stopped. I had no word from him for many weeks. Then one day his mother called to tell me they had been notified by the War Department that he was missing in action. She was a religious woman and said she was praying as hard as she knew how that he would be all right. She called me because Chuck had written to her saying that I was the girl he planned to marry. He had never told me that. The fact that the telegram said he was missing, not killed, was at least something to cling to. After that, I called her every week, eager to hear news, trying to bolster her spirits and mine. But I didn't have much hope. I figured Chuck was gone."

under his parachute. Just after dawn the next morning Yeager saw a woodcutter with an ax walking nearby. Prepared to kill the man if necessary to get the ax, he confronted him with pistol in hand. The frightened woodcutter was a Frenchman who seemed friendly. Yeager tried to tell the man he needed to make contact with the French underground (those who were resisting the Germans), but neither man spoke the other's language. Finally, with hand signals, the woodcutter told Yeager to remain hidden until he returned with someone who could speak English.

More than an hour later, Yeager heard footsteps approaching. He wondered whether the woodcutter had come back with a squad of German soldiers. With his heart pounding and his .45 at the ready, Yeager stayed in hiding until he heard a voice say, "American, a friend is here. Come out."[14]

Hiding in the Hay

The speaker was an older man who led the airman on a harrowing journey through the thickest part of the woods. Several times they stopped and hid as German patrols came near. Finally, they reached a stone farmhouse. There the old man showed Yeager to a hayloft in a barn and a tiny room used to store tools. After locking the American inside, he pitched hay against the door until it was no longer visible.

For a man of action like Yeager, the situation was almost intolerable. Feeling claustrophobic and drenched in sweat, he wondered whether the old man might have locked him inside just to turn him over to the Germans for a cash reward. That possibility seemed even more likely when he heard several men speaking German climbing the ladder to the hayloft. Years later Yeager recalled what happened next:

> My automatic is out, my finger on the trigger. The sounds are muffled but definite: they're rummaging in the hay, maybe stabbing into it with bayonets like a war movie. I don't know how long I sweat it out, but straining to hear, I hear nothing. I never hear them leave—if they have. Maybe they are just sitting out there, having a smoke, and playing a nasty game on me. . . . They come for me several hours later, I hear the sounds of hay being moved; by then, the .45 feels like it weighs 50 pounds and it takes both of my aching hands to hold it. Before he opens the door, the old man wisely whispers to me: "It's me. You're okay. They're gone."[15]

Yeager was then escorted into the farmhouse where he had his first meal in twenty-four hours. That night, a French doctor came by and removed shrapnel from his feet and hands. Then it was back out to that little room in the hayloft for almost a week.

At last, the doctor returned with civilian clothes and an ax intended to disguise the American as a French woodcutter. The two men set out on bicycles, traveling mostly at night and hiding in farmhouses during the day to avoid German patrols. At the village of Nerac Yeager was introduced to a farmer named Gabriel. For two weeks, he hid in one of Gabriel's sheds, eating meals with the family when it seemed safe. Made restless by inactivity, Yeager grew bored. This nearly proved disastrous one afternoon.

Sick of staying in the shed, he decided to sit out under a sycamore tree in the yard. Suddenly, without warning, a group of German soldiers marched by not ten feet from where he sat. Miraculously, they failed to recognize him as an American. Had his identity been revealed, he would surely have been captured and Gabriel shot immediately.

MOVING TOWARD FREEDOM

Yeager's boredom ended for good one evening when Gabriel led him deep into the pine forest. After a journey of two days, Gabriel asked Yeager to hide while he went on ahead alone. Many hours later he returned with a group of men carrying rifles and wearing black berets. These were the Maquis, the French resistance fighters. They hid by day and blew up trains and bridges by night. The plan was that Yeager would stay with the Maquis until the spring thaws in the Pyrenees. At that time they would help him cross over into Spain.

During his time with the Maquis he was in constant danger. If caught in civilian

French resistance fighters, known as the Maquis, helped Yeager escape into Spain after he was shot down over France.

clothes, he would probably have been tortured and then executed. Constantly on the move to avoid German patrols, the group of about twenty-five fighters never stayed in any one place for more than a day. Yeager would have liked to go on their missions, but since he could not speak French it was too dangerous. Instead, frustrated by his inability to do more, he was left behind with the cook and the camp guard.

He was finally able to make himself of use after the fighters received a secret airdrop from a British Royal Air Force plane. Among the food and ammunition were bundles of plastic explosives. Yeager had seen his father use similar explosives when he worked on the gas wells of West Virginia. When the Maquis realized Yeager had knowledge they could use in making their bombs, he was put in charge of making explosive fuse devices.

He said good-bye to the Maquis on a March morning when he was loaded into the back of a van and driven south. After a drive of several hours, he was transferred to another van with a pitch-black interior. Inside were four other downed fliers. They all realized that this was the moment they had been waiting for. They were on their way to the foothills of the Pyrenees where they would attempt to cross into Spain.

A DAUNTING CLIMB

Then a flashlight snapped on and a Frenchman who spoke English explained the situation. After distributing hand-drawn maps of the route they should take through the mountains, he told them that the trek would be rough and that, barring any blizzards, it would probably take four or five days of hard climbing to reach the border. They could travel together or pair off, but however they made the journey the most dangerous moments would be just before they crossed over into Spanish territory. Because the area was heavily patrolled by Germans a night crossing was preferable. Capture meant torture and execution.

Around midnight the truck braked to a stop in a heavily wooded area. The men were handed knapsacks of food and directed to a hut where they could spend the rest of the night. At first light, however, they would have to start climbing—there were German patrols about.

The date was March 23. With luck they would be in Spain by the end of the month. But the Pyrenees, whose highest peaks reach eleven thousand feet, are formidable mountains, and the Americans soon real-

ized that crossing them was going to be an ordeal that would take every ounce of their strength.

Yeager and a big man named Patterson who had been a navigator on a B-24 bomber were the strongest climbers. Around noon they reached the timberline well ahead of the other two men. After eating lunch and waiting in vain for the others to catch up, Yeager and Patterson pushed on alone.

Steep ridges and heavy, wet snow sapped their strength, and they had trouble breathing in the thin air. At night they tried to sleep under rock outcroppings, but by the fourth day they were exhausted and close to giving up. Because of clouds and fog they were unsure where they were. Late that afternoon they stumbled upon an abandoned cabin.

AWAKING TO GUNFIRE

Too tired to go on, they fell asleep inside on the bare wooden floor. Then, just before dark, a German patrol happened by and someone noticed the wet socks that Patterson had carelessly hung on a bush outside the cabin. Without even bothering to check inside, they began firing through the cabin door.

Yeager awoke to the whine of bullets. Without thinking, he dove out the rear window with Patterson right behind. As Patterson scrambled out the window, a bullet struck and nearly blew off his leg. Grabbing the big man, Yeager jumped onto a log flume (a kind of water slide used to move logs down the mountain). The two men tumbled and slid until the flume dumped them into an icy creek. By then Patterson was unconscious from loss of blood. Yeager scrambled to shore and then bandaged the stump of Patterson's leg with an extra shirt from his knapsack.

With night coming on and Germans close by, Yeager decided his only chance was to try to make it over the top and into Spain in the dark. Holding Patterson by the collar, he began dragging the unconscious man behind him as he inched up the steep, icy slopes. Every few yards he stopped to check Patterson's breathing to see if he was still alive.

But the navigator continued to breathe weakly. In the dark, Yeager pushed on, inching ever upward. At one point he slipped, and they slid backward down the hill some fifty feet, their momentum thank-fully stopped by a big boulder. The going was so difficult that Yeager began to think the unconscious Patterson was lucky.

Cursing the mountain and the situation, Yeager was simply too stubborn to give up. During his exertions he completely lost track of time and was genuinely surprised when the sky began to lighten and he found himself standing on a rocky ledge. Far below was a road that he knew had to be in Spain.

"Sledding" into Spain

His climbing was finally over, but now he had a new problem. How was he going to get the unconscious Patterson down the icy

---

Crawling and Hauling

Few men would have kept going the way Yeager did as he dragged his unconscious companion up a mountain in the dark. In his autobiography Yeager described the internal struggle that went on during that long night.

"I think, 'He's the lucky one. He's unconscious.' Every muscle in my body is hammering at me. I just want to let go . . . and drop in my tracks—either to sleep or to die. I don't know why I keep hold of him and struggle to climb. It's the challenge, I guess, and a stubborn pride knowing that most guys would've let go of Pat before now and before he stopped breathing. I keep going on anger, cursing the mountain that's trying to break my hump. The mountain isn't exactly trembling, but getting mad at it at least keeps my blood warmer. It's too dark to do anything but inch up, mostly crawling and hauling. I have no idea how far I am from the top, which is just as well, because if I did know I would probably quit right then and there. I decide not to stop and rest; I can't trust myself not to fall asleep and let go of Pat."

slope? Seeing no other option, Yeager carefully pushed Patterson's body over the edge and watched it careen down the mountain till it came to a stop. Yeager followed behind, sliding on his rear while holding a tree branch to use as a brake.

Alternating between pushing Patterson and sledding after him, Yeager eventually reached the side of the road. By then Patterson was so gray that Yeager thought he might be dead. Since there was nothing more he could do for the wounded airman, Yeager left him there and went looking for help. A passing motorist stopped for Patterson and took him to the nearest hospital. Despite his ordeal, he recovered from his wound and eventually returned to the States.

Meanwhile, Yeager walked on for what seemed like another twenty miles. Upon reaching a small village he turned himself in to the local police, who regarded the wild-looking Yeager as a suspicious character and locked him in a jail cell.

After all that he had endured, Chuck Yeager was not about to spend the night in captivity. Despite being so tired he would soon sleep for two days straight, he pulled a saw out of his survival kit and cut through the bars of the jail. Then he checked himself into a small hotel a few blocks away, ate a big meal, and went to bed. He was still sleeping when the American consul showed up outside his door. His ordeal over, Yeager now only had to wait while his government made arrangements to get him back to England.

4 The College of Life and Death: World War II Air Combat

Safe in neutral Spain by the end of March 1944, Yeager's struggles nevertheless were far from over. As soon as he finished the fight to gain his freedom, he began waging an unprecedented campaign to get back in the war. Military regulations then in force stated that no downed flier who successfully evaded capture would be sent back into combat. The reasoning for the so-called Evadee Rule was that a flier who survived being shot down and was captured a second time would undoubtedly be tortured by the Germans until he revealed how he had escaped the first time. That would endanger the lives of hundreds of people in the French underground. It was a sensible policy; only someone with the stubbornness of a Chuck Yeager would attempt to challenge it. After succeeding in his unlikely quest, Yeager rejoined the air war and quickly proved himself a force to be reckoned with. By the time the war ended there was little doubt that he was one of the best pilots in the world. And the poise and self-reliance he had displayed in and out of combat during the war years would serve him well afterward.

But before he could return to combat, Yeager first had to find his way back to England. It took six weeks for the Spanish government to grant permission for Yeager and five other downed airmen to be flown back to England. During that time, Yeager was not exactly roughing it:

> The American consul came up to Lierda, where we had gotten to, and put us up in a hotel, and gave us money and came to see us every week. We had the life of Reilly there; it was really neat. Then, finally, they gradually worked us down [south], then they made arrangements to deal with the Spanish government. Spain didn't have any gasoline and no way of getting it, so the U.S. government traded gasoline for the airmen that were interned in Spain.[16]

Yeager did little but eat good food, sunbathe on his hotel room balcony, and flirt with the hotel chambermaids. He returned to his squadron in mid-May to find his legend considerably enlarged.

Until then, no pilot who had been shot down had ever returned to Leiston. Yet here was Yeager, not only back from the dead, but tanned and well fed. Typically, he could not resist embellishing his story, making it sound as if he had been on a paid vacation while his buddies shivered and starved in chilly England.

THE FIGHT TO STAY ON

In truth, Yeager's reunion with his squadron was bittersweet. He was only there to pack his bags before returning to the States in June. But once at Leiston Yeager realized that this was where he wanted to be. He had never thought of himself as a quitter, and going back to the States where he would probably finish out the war as a flight instructor was not an appealing prospect.

After all those months of training, it just did not seem fair that he would not be able to use the skills he had acquired. Although the odds were heavily against him, he decided to fight his reassignment to the States. Yeager argued his case all the way up the chain of command. The officers he spoke with were amused to meet a junior officer who refused to go home. Although most were sympathetic, they explained that the regulations gave them no room to make an exception.

In June, a few days after the Allied invasion of France had begun, Yeager and a bomber captain who also did not want to be sent home had a brief meeting with General Dwight Eisenhower, the Supreme Commander of Allied forces in Europe, to plead their case.

> The only reason he saw us was just, I think, because he thought it a compliment to see somebody who didn't want to go home. He was a nice guy. He said, "I can't give you permission to go back on combat, because if you're shot down again, you compromise the underground system, but you go on back to your outfit and I'll go on back to the War Department, and ask for permission for me to make a decision.[17]

Returning to Leiston, Yeager kept any optimism in check. Meanwhile, while awaiting a final ruling, he was allowed to fly again—although only over England. He spent the next few weeks helping train replacement pilots by dogfighting with them. By this time, there were only a dozen pilots from his original squadron left at Leiston. All the rest had been killed, captured, or sent home.

GROUNDED!

Even in this relatively safe environment, Yeager had a way of finding trouble. One day, while dogfighting with three new pilots, he was diverted out over the North Sea to provide air cover for a couple of bomber crewman who had just been shot down. The men were bobbing in a dinghy, awaiting rescue by a patrol boat. While circling above them Yeager spotted a German fighter heading in their direction. Most likely it was coming out to strafe the downed crewman.

Impulsively, without telling anyone, Yeager broke away from the others and headed straight for the Junkers JU-88. Its pilot saw him coming and turned tail for German territory. Yeager caught him just as he reached the coastline and pumped several rounds into the enemy plane before it exploded into flames and crashed spectacularly on the beach.

Back at Leiston, Yeager found that his aggressive instincts had gotten him in deep trouble once again. His exasperated commanding officer called him into his office to remind Yeager that he had been under strict orders to avoid combat until his situation was clarified. In the meantime, he was grounded until further notice.

Two days later, Yeager feared the worst when he was ordered back into the squadron's operations office. To his surprise, instead of being yelled at again, he was handed a message rescinding his travel orders. General Eisenhower had been allowed to rule in his favor—he could now officially rejoin the war.

BACK IN ACTION

Yeager's successful battle to remain at Leiston mystified many of his fellow pilots. They could not understand why a man would willingly face death every day when he could go home for good. Most of them thought Yeager was crazy for not taking his Bronze Star (awarded for saving Patterson's life in the Pyrenees) and sitting out the rest of the war. But Yeager did not think that way.

This was where the action was, and in his gut he felt that this was where he belonged. It certainly was not a pleasant life. On mission days pilots got up around 5:30 A.M. for briefings that explained where they would rendezvous with the bombers they would escort deep into Germany. Breakfast was typically a piece of bread and a cup of coffee. Around eight in the morning the fighter pilots took off in their P-51 Mustangs. Already cold and tired, they knew

Yeager pleaded with General Dwight Eisenhower (pictured) to allow him to rejoin the war effort.

that they would be spending the next six hours in the air—if they were lucky. If they were unlucky, it might well be their last morning on Earth.

Typically, the fighters flew at thirty thousand feet. At that altitude the air temperature was around sixty degrees below zero. Since P-51 cabins were not

Once back in the war, Yeager became part of a squadron like this one that protected Allied bombers from attack by German fighters.

pressurized, the pilots were easily fatigued in the thin air. And the heaters were so inadequate that Yeager's left foot (the one farthest from the heater) usually froze while his right foot was comfortably warm.

The fighters' primary job was to protect Allied bombers from attacks by German fighters. Circling back and forth high above the bomber formations, they would dive on any enemy planes sent up to challenge the

attack. But during Yeager's first months back in the squadron there was little opportunity to engage enemy fighters. Few were sighted. It seemed as if the Germans were holding their forces back.

It was a frustrating time for Yeager because he was unable to use his considerable skills. Although he had been designated as one of the four squadron leaders who led the men into combat, he was the only squadron leader who was not an ace (a pilot who has shot down five or more enemy planes). Now a second lieutenant, he was also the lowest-ranking officer in the entire squadron, and the fact that he had been given a position of such responsibility bothered some of the higher-ranking pilots.

Yeager's leadership role did not bother his superiors, though. They respected his superior flying skills and legendary eyesight. Despite his lack of combat kills and lowly rank, they picked him to lead the entire group on a mission over Germany in October. Yeager was honored; with more than twenty aces in the entire 357th Fighter Group, he was the one chosen to lead this important mission.

An Ace in a Day

Being in the lead meant that he would have first crack at any enemy fighters. On October 12, while leading the group on a mission over Bremen, Germany, Yeager's luck finally changed. Some fifty miles off in the distance he spotted twenty-two specks. They were Me-109s, German fighters waiting for the Allied bombers to arrive over the city.

Nearly fifty years later, Yeager vividly recalled what happened next. The most dangerous moment occurred early in the fight. Just as he was shooting down one plane, the enemy's wingman tried to slip in behind him. It took a masterful bit of flying to turn the tables:

> But when I spotted them I moved around into the sun and they didn't see us. We came in behind them and just

overtook them . . . . I know they saw us, we were so close, and when I opened up this guy broke in mid-air collision with one of the others. . . . I pulled in behind a 109 and was hammering him, and his wingman cut the power back. I caught it out of the corner of my eye, and about the time my target blew up, I broke full right, cut the power way back, slapped the flaps down about 20 degrees and came around. I was really about 50 feet from that guy, I was decelerating, and all I did was move off his right wingtip, kick right rudder and open up. And man, that sawed that airplane in two. I'm sure I killed the pilot.[18]

A few moments later, Yeager chased another German fighter down in a steep dive. He was able to pull his P-51 up in time, but the 109 did not make it. It was Yeager's fifth kill of the day. (He was given credit for the two planes that collided when they first saw him.) After going almost eight months with only one kill, he had downed five planes in the space of about twenty minutes. That night at the officer's club at Leiston there was a big celebration. The squadron's "hillbilly" was finally an ace.

Meanwhile, word of the day's accomplishments spread quickly. Yeager was promoted to captain and recommended for a Silver Star, and the military newspaper *Stars and Stripes* published the story with an explanation of how General Eisenhower had interceded so that he could return to combat. The front-page headline read: FIVE KILLS VINDICATE IKE'S DECISION.

Sky Warriors

There were some basic rules that pilots who wanted to survive in combat learned very quickly. But, as Yeager explained in his autobiography, attitude was just as important.

"Dogfighting demanded the sum total of all your strengths, and exposed any of your weaknesses. Some good pilots lacked the eyes; others became too excited and lost concentration, or lost their nerve and courage; a few panicked in tight spots and did stupid things that cost them their lives. The best pilots were also the most aggressive, and it showed.

We quickly learned basic do's and don'ts. If the enemy was above, we didn't climb to meet him because we lost too much speed. When in a jam, we never ran. That was exactly what he expected. It was always important to check your back when popping out of the clouds: you could have jumped out in front of a 109. We avoided weaving around cumulus clouds; they're like boulders and you could have been easily ambushed. And we were particularly alert while flying beneath high thin cirrus clouds. Germans could look down through them and see you, but you couldn't see up through them. . . . We also tried to avoid overshooting an enemy plane, which put you in front of his gun-sights; it was like shooting yourself down. One of the guys once asked Colonel Spicer, our group commander, what to do if caught by a larger force. 'Rejoice, laddie,' the old man said, 'that's why you're here.'"

Hunting an Elusive Enemy

It would not be the last time Yeager was recommended for a medal. Near the war's end the Germans had developed a formidable new air weapon. Their newest twin-engine fighters were propelled by jet engines. Because they had a 150-mile-per-hour speed advantage on the propeller-driven P-51s, they would simply pull away out of range if approached. (They were under strict orders to concentrate their attacks only on Allied bombers.)

Despite the speed differential, Yeager could not resist trying to down one. One day, not long after a futile chase of three jets near Essen, Germany, he was flying over a German airfield when he spotted a jet coming in for a landing far below. Despite the presence of numerous antiaircraft guns, he dove on the jet, hoping to get a few clean shots before making a getaway. With flak exploding all around, he fired one accurate burst that ripped into the jet's wings. As Yeager spun up and away, the jet crash-landed short of the runway. For his daring on this occasion, he was recommended for a Distinguished Flying Cross.

By the last week of November, Yeager was an ace two times over. He scored his tenth kill during one of the largest dogfights in history. It occurred during a mission to destroy underground fuel facilities near Poznan, Poland. A number of Mustangs had been specially fitted so that they

German airmen parachute from their doomed plane. Yeager became a flying ace in one day by shooting down five German planes.

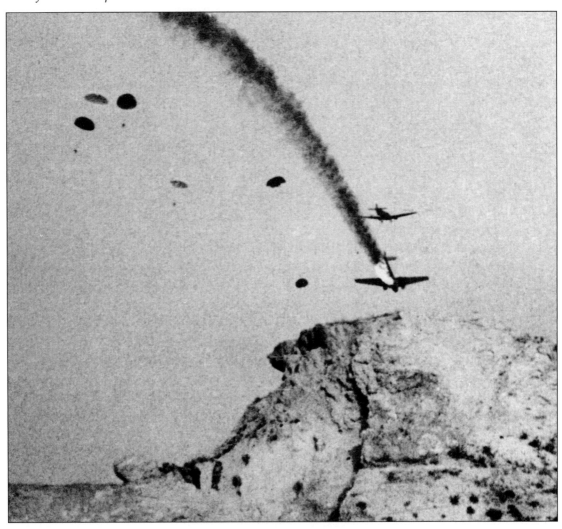

could carry bombs, and Yeager was in another group of fighters assigned to fly cover for the bomb-carrying Mustangs.

Mistaking the loaded Mustangs for a fleet of unescorted heavy bombers, the Germans sent up every available fighter plane in Germany and Poland. As usual, Yeager and his best friend, fellow pilot Clarence "Bud" Anderson, were the first to see a mass of at least 150 German fighters. As the cloud of German planes approached, the 16 Mustangs in Yeager's squadron prepared for battle. They did not know it at the time, but the Germans had sent up a total of some 750 fighter planes against 200 Mustangs.

Almost immediately, Yeager shot down two planes. Then he lost track of time as hundreds of planes looped and dived through the skies, each pilot fighting for his life. When the kill-or-be-killed drama finally ended, *Glamorous Glennis* was still flying—and the ground below was littered with burning planes. Ninety-eight of the downed planes were German, while the Allies lost only eleven.

SAYING GOOD-BYE TO EUROPE

That battle proved to be one of the last big contests in an air war that was winding down fast, as was Yeager's tour of duty. He was due to come home in January 1945. At the end of November 1944 he and the three other men still left from the original thirty in their squadron celebrated one year at Leis-

DUTY, DISCIPLINE, AND DEATH

A sense of duty and the discipline to concentrate totally on the job at hand are two of Chuck Yeager's most notable character traits. In this excerpt from an interview published in Aviation History *in May of 1998 he noted how those traits not only served him in combat, but led to future successes as a test pilot.*

"And that's probably been the whole story of my life; I was always faced with a job to do where duty became paramount. In combat you learn real quick that if you don't have any control over the outcome of a situation, forget it. Concentrate on what you're doing. Just stay out of that death arena, and that's exactly the way we went through it, and I was disciplined that way. Sure, guys were getting killed on missions, but you never gave any thought to it 'cause you don't have any control over it.

[Years later] they said, 'Did you think you'd be able to break the sound barrier?' It didn't make any difference whether I thought I could or not. I had to try, because that's my duty. And consequently, it was easy for me to transition into research flying because of my discipline in combat."

ton. Yeager had flown a total of sixty-four combat missions and survived his harrowing experience. It was sobering to realize that twenty of their fellow pilots had either been killed or were missing in action. Only six had actually finished their tour of duty.

A few weeks before he was due to be sent home, Yeager was unexpectedly sent to Geneva, Switzerland. Because of his experiences in the Pyrenees, someone thought he might be able to help plan the escapes of downed fliers who had made it to neutral Switzerland. Nothing came of those plans, but he did get a nice vacation out of it.

Finally, on January 15, 1945, Yeager and Bud Anderson flew their last combat mission. They were flying as backups for any Mustangs on the assigned mission who might develop engine problems after crossing the English Channel. When none did, Yeager and Anderson went off by themselves for a little unauthorized sightseeing.

First they flew to Switzerland, where Yeager pointed out the Lake Geneva hotel where he had stayed. Switzerland, however, was a neutral country and the fact that they were doing their sightseeing at five hundred miles per hour and only a few feet off the ground probably would have got them court-martialed if anyone could have figured out who they were. Yeager then flew on to the south of France to see if he could trace his escape route. He flew over the farmhouses and sheds where he had hidden and even the shack in the Pyrenees where the Germans had nearly killed him and his partner.

On their way back to Leiston, the two retiring warriors made a side trip to Paris. They buzzed the Arc de Triomphe and then headed back to England, landing at six in the evening.

"We'd just shot up a mountain in a neutral country, buzzed half of Europe, and probably could have been court-martialed on any one of a half-dozen charges," recalled Bud Anderson. "It didn't matter. We were aglow. It was over, we had survived, we were finished, and now we would go home together."[19]

Although their war was over, they had been changed forever. As Yeager put it in his autobiography,

> We were a pack of untested kids who grew up in a hurry. Andy called it the college of life and death. I don't recommend going to war as a way of testing character, but by the time our tour ended we felt damned good about ourselves and what we had accomplished. Whatever the future held, we knew our skills as pilots, our ability to handle stress and danger, and our reliability in tight spots. It was the difference between thinking you're pretty good, and proving it.[20]

Chapter

5 Hog Heaven

Most young American servicemen returned home from World War II to settle down and begin raising a family. Only twenty-two when the fighting ended, Captain Chuck Yeager also planned on doing those things. But it would be an exaggeration to say that he actually settled down. As unlikely as it seemed, he soon found himself doing more dangerous flying than ever. And the skills he had learned during combat put him in the forefront of a new era of supersonic aviation.

Still, when he and his best friend, Bud Anderson, left England for good in February of 1945, three months before the end of the war in Europe, neither man was thinking much about his long-term future. After a year of combat both were intent on marrying the girls waiting for them back home. Yeager was so focused on reuniting with Glennis that, upon arriving from Europe, he bypassed West Virginia and took a train directly to California. Once there, he asked Glennis to accompany him back East to meet his family and get married. Although she was only twenty, Glennis had no doubt that this was the man she wanted to marry.

On the train back to West Virginia the two talked about a future with the air corps. When Hamlin's war hero and his bride-to-be arrived, the little town threw them a big parade. Then, on February 26, 1945, they were married in the family's parlor. After the wedding they boarded a train for Del Mar, California, where the air corps maintained a rest and recreation center for soldiers on leave. They planned to spend the next two weeks honeymooning beside the ocean. Yeager got a delightful surprise when they went down to the beach. The first person he ran into was Bud Anderson and *his* new bride.

UNHAPPY IN TEXAS

Like Yeager, Anderson had been assigned to Perrin Field in Texas. When the honeymoon ended, the two couples headed for Texas. It turned out to be an unpleasant assignment. Older officers who had spent the war in Texas did not look favorably on the two cocky combat veterans who seemed to have been promoted beyond their years. (Yeager was a twenty-two-year-old captain and Anderson a twenty-three-year-old major.)

They were given jobs as student pilot instructors, an assignment that, after the dan-

In this famous photograph, a sailor kisses a woman on a New York City street in jubilation at the news that the war is over.

gers of combat flying, provided few thrills. Anderson put it this way:

> To break the monotony, Chuck and I would take up some students, meet someplace, take over the controls from the back seat, and dogfight with one another. Sometimes we got carried away. Once, Chuck blew a side panel out of his canopy in a dive. I don't know what the students thought. We probably

scared them to death. After a year of life-and-death flying, we were simply bored stiff.[21]

At the same time Glennis was experiencing a difficult pregnancy with the Yeagers' first child. Then Yeager got one of the luckiest breaks of his life. The army issued a new regulation allowing former prisoners of war or evadees to select an assignment at the base of their choice. It was a way out of an intolerable situation in Texas, and with Glennis not feeling well, Yeager decided it would be wise to find a base close to Hamlin so his family could help out if necessary.

The base nearest to Hamlin turned out to be Wright Field in Dayton, Ohio. Al-though Yeager picked it with Glennis's health in mind, it turned out to be the perfect place for a fighter pilot who craved excitement. It was July of 1945 when Yeager reported for duty at Wright Field. His background in maintenance and his unquestioned flying abilities earned him a position as the assistant maintenance officer of the fighter test section of the flight test division. Because there was no family housing available anywhere near Dayton, Glennis settled with Chuck's parents in Hamlin. Yeager came down on weekends whenever he could, but often he was far too busy flying. He wrote Glennis one night, telling her, "I miss you, hon, but I'm in hog heaven."[22]

A HOTSHOT HITS THE JACKPOT

In an interview for Aviation History *on the fiftieth anniversary of his breaking of the sound barrier, Chuck Yeager talked about the good fortune that allowed him to escape from an assignment as a flight instructor in Texas to a job that allowed him to fly the hottest new planes nearly every day.*

"Well, I came back home, made basic instructor in the summer of '45. The war ended in Europe, all of the POWs were released and all of the airmen, pilots, navigators, bombardiers and gunners who had been shot down and either evaded or were prisoners of war could select any air base in the United States and the Air Force would assign them there. That was a gift. And I said, man, that includes me, 'cause I was an evadee and I was an instructor in T-6s at Perrin Field, Texas. The closest air base to my home was Wright Field, and I asked for it. They assigned me there. When I reported in, the personnel guys looked at my records. I was a 22-year-old fighter pilot, I had about 1,200 hours in P-39s and P-51s, but the thing that caught their eye was that I was a maintenance officer. . . . There was an opening in the fighter test section for a maintenance officer, and that's where they assigned me. It was just pure luck."

THE WRIGHT PLACE

He was in hog heaven because, as a maintenance officer, he could fly hot new planes almost anytime he wanted in the course of his duties. A mere two weeks after arriving at Wright, he was flying a Lockheed P-80 Shooting Star, the nation's first operational jet fighter, at 550 miles per hour, faster than he had ever gone in a P-51. Typically, he loved the sensation. Over the next decade most of the nation's military planes would be making the transition from propeller-driven to jet-powered flight. The Flight Performance School at Wright Field, the initial name of the U.S. Air Force Test Pilot School, was the premier training ground for the newest planes, and Yeager was at the heart of the action.

Twenty-five fighter test pilots were stationed at Wright. They were involved in the kind of dangerous and exciting work that Yeager loved, but he never thought he had a chance of becoming a test pilot himself. After all, those men were all college-educated and most had engineering degrees. Still, he had plenty of opportunity to indulge his love of flying. While assigned to Wright, Yeager flew at least twenty-five different kinds of planes, including captured German and Japanese aircraft. He was in the air six to eight hours a day—whenever a plane was repaired the maintenance officer checked it out in flight before it could be flown again. Those early jet engines broke down frequently, so it was not long before Yeager was the most experienced jet pilot in the entire air corps.

And his curiosity was boundless. Unlike most of the other test pilots, he was fasci-nated by the various systems of the aircraft he flew. Not only did he want to learn how a plane handled but why it handled the way it did. If there was a switch on the instrument panel, he needed to understand its function. Airplanes were his passion, and without consciously trying, he was gaining more practical knowledge about them than nearly anyone else in the world.

That knowledge would prove invaluable when he got into trouble thousands of feet in the air. He had an instinctive feel for how a plane should fly, and his mechanical aptitude often allowed him to sense which particular system was malfunctioning. His abilities caught the eye of Colonel Albert Boyd, the head of the air corps's flight test division. To the irritation of the other test pilots, Boyd begin giving more and more responsibility to the "uneducated" hillbilly who, some felt, should stick to his maintenance duties.

A TRIP TO THE DESERT

Because those early jet engines were so un-reliable, a safer place was needed to test them. That was why, in August of 1945, Boyd, a detachment of test pilots, and Yeager were temporarily sent to remote Muroc Army Air Field (now Edwards Air Force Base) in the Mojave Desert about seventy miles northeast of Los Angeles. The dried lakebeds there were eight miles long, the perfect place to test the Shooting Star jet. As maintenance officer, Yeager was busy keeping a half-dozen planes in the air.

When the tests were over, one of the planes had to be flown back to Wright Field. Over the objections of the test pilots

Yeager waves from the cockpit of his plane. After World War II ended, Yeager became a fighter test pilot.

who felt one of them should be assigned the job, Boyd chose Yeager. The West Virginian appreciated the colonel's confidence in him. He was still self-conscious about his lack of formal education—even though he could fly rings around most of the other fighter test pilots. He challenged them to dogfights every chance he got, but won so often that they refused to fly against him.

One of the few other pilots whose flying ability he respected was a man named Bob Hoover. Like Yeager, Hoover was not an official test pilot but had plenty of experience flying combat in World War II. He was about the only other pilot who had the skills to dogfight with Yeager. Because of their similar background and love of flying, the two men became close friends.

"Aladdin's Lamp with Unlimited Rubs"

Yeager reported to Wright Field in July of 1945 and, as he noted in Yeager: An Autobiography, *he was delighted with the situation he found there.*

"I had eleven hundred hours of flying time and a background in maintenance. I was a perfect candidate for what they needed: a fighter pilot to run functional test flights on all the airplanes after engine overhauls and other repairs. I was assigned as an assistant maintenance officer to the fighter test section of the flight test division, the hub, over the next decade, for the testing of a radically new generation of powerful airplanes that would take us to the edge of space and change aviation forever. These tremendous changes occurred in the age of the slide rule, before computers were born or advanced wind tunnels existed. We would discover by dangerous trial and error what worked and what didn't. That cost lives, but for the pilots who survived, it was the most thrilling time imaginable. I was in on the beginning of the Golden Age. Two weeks after arriving at Wright, I was flying the first operational American jet fighter.

I had no idea of what the future might hold when I reported in. All I knew was that Wright Field was a fun place to be, loaded with every airplane in the inventory, and there was plenty of gasoline. It was like Aladdin's lamp with unlimited rubs. I could fly as much as I wanted, building flying experience on dozens of different kinds of fighters. The first chance I got I flew to Hamlin and buzzed Glennis. I called her that night and said, 'I miss you, hon, but I'm in hog heaven.'"

Yeager was in "hog heaven" as a test pilot at Wright Field in 1945.

In his autobiography, *Forever Flying*, Hoover described the paradoxical situation he and Yeager found themselves in at Wright Field:

> Flying as a test pilot was just as dangerous as flying combat, but in a different way. Fighter pilots are trained to believe that they are the best pilots flying the best planes. They must believe they can outwit and out perform the enemy in life-and-death encounters. . . . Test pilots also face life-threatening situations. Flying experimental aircraft is by definition trial and error. Yet, test pilots cannot afford to make errors.[23]

BARNSTORMING IN THE JET AGE

The friendship between Hoover and Yeager grew in the fall of 1945 when they were assigned to do air shows together around the country. Such shows were quite popular after the war. People wanted to see the newest military planes in action.

"While many of the senior officers at Wright Field weren't interested in barnstorming around the country, Chuck and I were," recalled Bob Hoover. "We traveled to such places as New York, Alabama, Wisconsin, and Oklahoma, where we performed our loops and spins for thousands of people."[24]

There were no hard and fast rules about what they could do. Men like Yeager and Hoover loved that kind of freedom and the opportunity to have some harmless fun. They put on entertaining shows, flying fast and low and trying all kinds of acrobatic stunts—including rocketing down the main streets of small towns.

Few Americans had ever seen a jet plane, and fewer yet understood how one worked. Many wondered how they could possibly fly without a propeller. The situation appealed to Yeager's mischievous sense of humor. With his plane parked in front of the

PUSHING THE LIMITS

Joe Lynch, an outstanding test pilot who was eventually killed in an accident at Nellis Air Force Base, was interviewed for a magazine called Skyline *in the early 1950s. In the article, which was quoted in Bob Hoover's* Forever Flying, *Lynch succinctly summed up the role of any test pilot.*

"Our job is to run engines and airplanes as hard as anyone says they can be run. This sometimes includes flying the plane to its breaking point and then bringing it back so it can be studied, and its automatic recording instruments interpreted. The number of things we do to test a plane is almost endless, and new things are always coming up."

grandstand, he would ask a volunteer to stand safely behind the tailpipe and light a newspaper. Just as it flared up he would ignite his engine and fire would shoot out the back. To those who did not know better, it looked as if the volunteer had lit the engine like the burner on a gas stove.

At another air show Yeager met a woman pilot who was doing stunts in a P-39. When she learned that Yeager loved flying the P-39 (he had not flown one since his training days in Nevada), and would do anything to do so again, they worked out a scheme. Yeager, dressed in a woman's wig and a white jump suit, did her air show, putting on a spectacular display of loops and spins. When he was done, he landed far enough away from the crowd so they could switch places and no one would be the wiser.

A FATEFUL QUESTION

Stunts like that were typical in those free-wheeling early days. Yet through it all, Yeager was increasing his flying skills. Toward the end of 1945 Colonel Boyd called Yeager into his office and asked him if he would like to be a test pilot. Although intrigued by the idea, Yeager was afraid his lack of education ruled him out. Boyd reassured him that he had the ability to make it through test pilot school.

In January 1946, Yeager and his friend Bob Hoover were enrolled in the test pilot school at Wright Field. The six-month program was split between actual flying and course work. The flying was no problem for Yeager, but the course work was another matter. Students were required to use algebra and calculus to make graphs and charts. Fortunately, a very bright student named Jack Ridley took Yeager under his wing and explained the mathematics for him in a way that Yeager could understand. Although he did not excel in the classroom portion of the school, he did well enough, combined with his exceptional flying ability, to pass.

One test flight, however, besides nearly getting him killed, almost got him bounced out of the service. He and an instructor were running a power-speed test in a two-seat T-6 trainer when the engine malfunctioned and they lost power rapidly. Looking for a place to put the plane down, Yeager made for a plowed farm field, but landed too close to the end. The plane skidded through a farmer's yard, blasted through a chicken coop, and hit a smokehouse before spinning to a stop in front of the farmhouse. When he finally came to a stop, Yeager was looking at the farmer's astonished wife through her kitchen window.

Under the circumstances, putting that T-6 down safely had been an incredible bit of flying. But it did not keep Yeager out of hot water. Since civilian property had been damaged, a board of inquiry was held. One of the crash's witnesses was a councilman who claimed that Yeager had buzzed down a nearby town's main street just before the crash. The officers who ran the inquiry asked some tough questions of Yeager. He sensed that they would have liked nothing better than to have him court-martialed.

A REPRIEVE

Yeager wondered whether his days as a military pilot were over. Fortunately, the testing equipment he had taken along for the flight provided a flight record that could be checked. The records confirmed that the T-6 had done nothing wrong—it was exactly where it was supposed to be when the accident occurred. Yeager was cleared of any wrongdoing and allowed to continue his training.

Meanwhile, back in Hamlin, Glennis gave birth to their first son, Donald, in the spring of 1946. Unable to be there because of the hearing, Yeager could only celebrate with Glennis over the phone. When he fi-nally got to hold Donald, he claimed it was one of the greatest moments in his life. Still, being away from family during important moments was typical for a military pilot. Both Yeager and his wife knew that that was a fact of life in the military.

Still, neither would have guessed that life was about to grow even more hectic. A few months after Yeager's June graduation from test pilot school, Colonel Boyd called him into his office. The outcome of that fateful meeting ensured that Chuck Yeager's name would go down in aviation history.

6 Riding the Bullet: The X-1

As a brand new test pilot outranked by almost all his fellow test pilots at Wright Field, Yeager had no expectation that he would get the choicest assignments. That did not particularly bother him since, no matter what, he would be flying. Yet, only a few months later, he was chosen above everyone else for an extremely dangerous assignment—an assignment that, if carried through to completion, would have him flying higher and faster than any human in history. There was little doubt that it would also make him famous.

Thoughts of fame were the last thing on his mind, however, when Colonel Boyd sent for him one day in the spring of 1947. Yeager figured he was in hot water for a prank he and some friends had pulled a few days earlier. Colonel Boyd had just bought a new car and Yeager and some other pilots had been unable to resist hiding pebbles in the hubcaps. Then they watched (and laughed) in secret as the puzzled colonel attempted to figure out where the noise was coming from.

Yeager suspected that someone had revealed that he was one of the pranksters and he anticipated trouble; Boyd had a reputation as an officer who would not tolerate foolishness. As Bob Hoover once said, "A no-nonsense, tough-as-nails career soldier, Boyd was never one to mince words."[25] Yeager's fears increased when he was made to stand at attention for nearly half an hour. Gradually, however, his fears abated when he realized that he was not there for a reprimand. Instead, he was being assessed as to whether he was the right man for a mission of crucial importance to the air corps.

Although the military had drawn up plans for many different kinds of new supersonic planes, development could not go forward until someone proved it was actually possible to fly faster than sound. In 1947 no aircraft had ever broken the so-called sound barrier. Many aviation authorities believed it was physically impossible.

An Invisible Wall?

Yeager's own experiences suggested that they might be right. During World War II, whenever he reached speeds in excess of five hundred miles per hour in his P-51 Mustang, the whole plane shook violently and the controls became almost impossible to operate. Planes that went into power

Geoffrey De Havilland poses next to his aircraft. De Havilland died trying to break the sound barrier in 1947.

land Jr. early in 1947 did nothing to dispel the notion. De Havilland had set out to become the first human to break the sound barrier, but during a practice dive at .94 Mach, his plane was ripped apart in midair.

Complicating the matter, the speed of sound varied depending on the density of the atmosphere. At sea level it was 760 miles per hour. Up in the thin air some forty thousand feet above the ground, it was only 660 miles per hour. That was one reason the rocket-powered experimental plane known as the X-1 had been designed to fly at higher altitudes than anyone had ever attempted.

Yeager had seen the X-1 a couple of times on his trips to Muroc. Since it was painted bright orange it was hard to miss. He had been much too busy with his own duties, however, to give much thought to the little bullet-shaped plane designed by the Bell Aircraft Corporation. That shape was no accident—Bell engineers had noted that bullets were one of the few things in the real world that traveled at supersonic speeds.

Bell had built the X-1 under a contract with the Army Air Corps. Until the summer of 1947, Bell had hired its own civilian pilots to test its experimental aircraft. Bell's principal test pilot, Chalmers "Slick" Goodlin, had taken the X-1 up to .8 Mach, before asking to renegotiate his contract. He felt the danger justified asking for in-

dives always ran into this kind of turbulence. The phenomenon led to a widespread belief that there was an invisible "sound barrier" that would tear a plane apart as it approached the speed of sound (also known as Mach 1). The death of famous British test pilot Geoffrey De Havil-

creased pay of $150,000. Until the matter was settled, he refused to fly.

A Supersonic Invitation

Losing patience with the delay, the Army Air Corps decided that it would provide the pilot. That was why Colonel Boyd called Yeager into his office. He had a strong hunch that Yeager was the man for the job, but wanted to confirm his intuition. When he asked Yeager why he had volunteered to fly the X-1, Yeager told him that it sounded interesting.

"Yeager," he noted emphatically, "this is *the* airplane to fly. The first pilot who goes faster than sound will be in the history books. It will be the most historic ride since the Wright brothers."[26]

Boyd then made sure Yeager understood both the danger and the responsibility.

THE TOUGHEST DECISION

Shortly before his death in 1976, Major General Albert Boyd was asked why he chose Chuck Yeager to fly the X-1. His explanation was included in Yeager: An Autobiography.

"Selecting the X-1 pilot was one of the most difficult decisions of my life. If the pilot had an accident, he could set back our supersonic program a couple of years.

. . . To me, Chuck was the ideal candidate, and I still feel that way twenty-seven years later. We had several other outstanding pilots to choose from, but none of them could quite match his skill in a cockpit or his coolness under pressure. About the only negative was his lack of a college education. That placed me in defensive position, if my superiors would ever second-guess me—but, fortunately, they didn't. Jack Ridley provided the engineering backup for Chuck, and those two were so close that we knew Chuck would rely heavily on Jack. I've never seen anyone who could explain engineering concepts better than Ridley, who was one helluva engineer and a test pilot himself.

I really did sweat out the crew selection, but in the end I felt we had the best group available to try to do what many thought was impossible. Over the years, I've often been asked if Chuck were the only one who could've successfully flown the X-1. I don't know, but I can't think of anyone who could've done a better job."

This would be the Army Air Corps' first crack at research flying, and a failure could well be disastrous. He then asked Yeager whom he would choose as backup pilot and flight engineer if he were picked to fly the X-1. Yeager named his friends and fellow test pilots, Bob Hoover and Jack Ridley. Shortly thereafter the three men were on their way to the Bell plant in Buffalo, New York, for a close look at the X-1.

For Yeager and his friends, the whole situation seemed unreal. Despite being 3 of the youngest junior test pilots of a group of 125 top test pilots, they were the ones being considered for an aviation milestone that would rival the Wright brothers' flight. By passing over so many pilots with more se-

Yeager stands ready in front of an X-1A. Yeager understood the danger involved in testing new planes.

niority and education, Boyd was taking a huge risk. If these young men failed he would face plenty of blame.

A "MONSTER" IN CHAINS

According to Hoover, their first encounter with the X-1 was unsettling:

> Chuck and I saw the plane for the first time up at Bell, and it was a pretty awesome experience for the two of us. They showed us what liquid oxygen was like. They took a rubber ball and put it in the liquid oxygen and then dropped it on the floor. It shattered. They did the same thing with a frog, and I'll tell you, that got our attention. Then they made the engine run for us. The airplane was log-chained in a building, and when the rockets were fired, the ceiling started cracking and breaking loose and falling on us, and I'd never been so scared in my life. It was just absolutely deafening. I think Pard [Yeager] was thinking the same thing I was: What are we getting ourselves into?[27]

They were also struck by how small the plane was—thirty-one feet long with a wingspan of only twenty-seven feet—and by its razor-thin wings. Despite its size, there was thirteen thousand pounds of fuel crammed inside. With a dozen different fuel containers packed into the fuselage, it was little more than a flying bomb—a fire or an explosion would be fatal. As test pilots, they also could not fail to notice that the only exit from the cockpit was through a side door that would position the pilot to be cut in half by the plane's wing. Despite

the obvious dangers, there was something about the X-1 that excited them.

All three men had a sense that they were about to be involved in a historic event. Hoover (who at one time had hoped to be the primary pilot for the X-1) now felt excitement rather than disappointment that he would not actually be in the pilot's seat:

> Colonel Boyd asked for our impressions when we returned to Wright Field. We probably sounded like kids who had been to an amusement park. An adventure of a lifetime was about to occur. I knew I had in all likelihood missed the chance to experience the thrill firsthand, but nevertheless I would have a front-row seat to history in the making.[28]

BEGINNING THE GREAT ADVENTURE

When Colonel Boyd asked Yeager what he thought about the plane, the response was typically direct. "Sir," he marveled, "that's the most tremendous airplane I've ever seen."[29] When the three men confirmed they were still interested, Boyd gave his final approval. Early in July of 1947, Yeager, Hoover, and Ridley were on their way to Muroc Army Air Field in California's Mojave Desert. They arrived on July 27, the day after President Truman signed the Armed Forces Unification Act, a law that created the modern air force as a service branch separate from the army and navy.

Muroc had no facilities for the families of men working on the X-1, and since the assignment was considered temporary, funds were not allotted for off-base housing. Despite the financial strain Yeager wanted his family with him. In their two years of marriage, Chuck and Glennis had lived together only a couple of months. They were tired of the constant separations. Away on an assignment earlier that year, Yeager had even missed the birth of his second son, Mickey.

After an intensive search, he and Glennis found a guesthouse for rent on a ranch some thirty miles from the base. Now, at least, Yeager could go home to his family after risking his life in the air. Not long after they arrived, he brought Glennis to the base to show her the X-1. Just as with his fighter plane in World War II, he had her name painted on the nose. He told his wife that she would always be his good luck charm.

From the Belly of a B-29

Not until August 1947 did Yeager actually fly the X-1—and even then it was a flight without power. The idea was that he needed to get a feel for the controls before trying powered flight. However, a flight without power was still a dangerous undertaking. To save all its precious fuel for the assault on the speed record, the X-1 was not designed to take off from the ground. Instead, it was hauled aloft hanging in the bomb bay of a B-29 bomber, then dropped at an altitude of twenty thousand feet or more.

For his first glide in the X-1 Yeager rode to the drop site in the B-29 sitting on an apple box behind the cockpit. His buddy Jack Ridley was the B-29's copilot, and Bob

Hoover flew nearby in a chase plane. It was too dangerous to get into the X-1 on the ground because there was always a chance the B-29 might have to drop the experimental plane if trouble arose. The B-29 climbed at only 180 miles per hour, and the X-1 stalled (failed to provide lift) at anything less than 240 miles per hour. A pilot inside an X-1 released during the bomber's climb would be unable to fly the plane; he would simply drop like a stone to the desert floor.

Just getting into the X-1 from the B-29 was one of the scariest moments of any flight. With plenty of open space between the two planes and a fifty-below-zero wind whistling past at close to two hundred miles per hour, the test pilot had to gingerly climb down a flimsy ladder to the cockpit. Designed to drop down under the pilot's weight, the ladder slid on some tracks. But the icy cold at high altitude caused the mechanism to stick. Often Yeager had to jump up and down on it before it fell with a sickening lurch.

Once the ladder was down, in his bulky pressure suit he had to somehow open the cockpit door with one hand while keeping a grip on the ladder with the other. Then he had to contort himself through the opening while hurricane-strength winds threatened to blow him out into empty space. He always breathed a sign of relief upon reaching the relative safety of the cockpit.

Bonding with the X-1

After the nerve-wracking entry, actually flying the X-1 was almost a relief. Those first unpowered glides in early August went ex-

A Douglas Skyrocket launches from a B-29 in 1951. Yeager launched the X-1 from the belly of a B-29.

tremely well. Without even thinking, Yeager began his first glide with two slow rolls. In almost total silence (his breathing was the only sound) he tried the plane's controls and found them delightfully light to the touch. The plane was so graceful and responsive that he was actually sorry when the flight ended some three minutes later.

That first flight made a strong impression on Herb Hoover, the chase plane pilot who witnessed it. In a letter to a friend, Hoover wrote, "This guy Yeager is pretty much of a wild one, but believe he'll be good on the Army ship. . . . On first drop, he did a couple of rolls right after leaving the B-29"![30]

Afterward, Yeager told anyone who would listen that the X-1 was the best airplane he had ever flown. On his second flight he found that it was so stable in a glide that he could fly it with both hands off the wheel. On his third and final glide test he even had a dogfight with Hoover as they spiraled down to the desert floor. Even without power the agile X-1 was more than a match for Hoover's F-80.

The first powered flight was scheduled for August 29. The plan was to take the plane up to .82 Mach, then go upward in increments of fifteen or twenty miles per hour in succeeding flights until the sound barrier was reached. Although Yeager and Ridley were enthusiastic, Colonel Boyd cautioned them against overconfidence.

UNCHAINING THE BEAST

Dick Frost, the engineer and former test pilot directing the Bell Company's X-1 program, was flying a chase plane on the day of the first powered flight. He instructed Yeager to fire only one rocket engine at a time (there were four) for five seconds at a time in order to keep the X-1 near the target speed of .82 Mach. At the end of the flight Yeager was supposed to fly by the Muroc tower at five thousand feet. Some high-ranking officers had flown out from Wright Field to observe the plane in flight. As it turned out, the brash young test pilot provided much more of a show than anyone could have imagined.

At twenty-one thousand feet the X-1 dropped from the B-29's bomb bay. Blinded for a moment by the bright sun, Yeager waited nearly fifteen seconds before igniting the engine chamber. He was slammed back against his seat as the plane surged forward. As planned he turned each cham-

Yeager smiles from the cockpit of a jet. The pilot described the X-1 as the best airplane he had ever flown.

Some Grueling Experiments

The X-1 was designed to fly at heights and speeds never before attempted by humans. In Forever Flying, *Bob Hoover recalled how he and Yeager had the unpleasant duty of serving as guinea pigs for the new equipment that would be needed to keep a human alive in that environment.*

"From the day Chuck was selected, we became an inseparable team. That included being involved in a number of bizarre experiments that the National Advisory Committee on Aeronautics (NACA), which later became the National Aeronautics and Space Administration (NASA), medical team felt warranted. They tested the limits of human endurance in the high-altitude pressure chamber and under high *g* [gravity] loads on the centrifuge.

Chuck and I were locked in altitude test chambers and strapped on to various centrifuges. . . . We wore bulky, tight-fitting capstan pressure suits that looked like something a primitive deep-sea diver would wear.

. . . That equipment exposed us to high *g*'s to determine our level of tolerance before blackout and unconsciousness. Even today, I can remember the nausea I experienced from twisting around on the centrifuges. Those were brutal experiments.

They would lock us in a sealed chamber and then simulate flight at eighty thousand feet. On one occasion, the chamber technician neglected to open the valve on my oxygen supply. My face turned morning-glory purple. Chuck Yeager loves to tell that story, and it seems funny now, but at the time I was petrified. I can't express the helpless feeling of having your lungs locked in the middle of a breath unable to inhale or exhale.

I almost choked to death. If Chuck had not looked through the porthole window at that particular instant, I would have been asphyxiated."

ber on and off in sequence in reaching a speed of a little over .8 Mach.

However, the slow roll he instinctively performed in the middle of that sequence was not part of the program. "My God," cried Frost in alarm, "that's not in the flight plan!"[31] Frost knew the maneuver might disrupt the fuel flow to the engines. It did, but power was quickly restored when Yeager returned the X-1 to an upright position.

Soon after, Frost had something much more pressing to worry about. Noticing that Yeager was diving at excessive speed toward the desert floor, he called out, "Hey! Where are you going now?"[32]

"To show those brass down there a real airplane!"[33] was the determined reply. At twenty-seven hundred feet above the desert, Yeager streaked by the Muroc control tower, pointed the X-1 skyward and fired all four chambers in sequence. Standing on an enormous tail of flame, the X-1 rocketed straight up before its astounded audience, reaching thirty-five thousand feet and .85 Mach before running out of fuel.

NEVER FEAR—THE AIR FORCE IS HERE!

Yeager's performance that day made it emphatically clear that, under the air force, the X-1 program would literally be moving faster than ever before. On his very first powered flight, he had reached .85 Mach and thirty-five thousand feet. Although his feat was a source of pride to the air force, the manner in which he accomplished it might well have caused him to be thrown out of the service. Trying to summarize the inexplicable impulse that had come over him, Yeager wrote to a former flying buddy: "I was so darned excited, scared, and thrilled (you know, that first-kill-in-Germany feeling) I couldn't say a word until the next day."[34]

Right after the flight when Frost called Larry Bell to tell him what had happened, Bell could only laugh and say, "Wait until Al Boyd hears about this. . . . He'll either pin a medal on that boy or give him hell."[35] Colonel Boyd had mixed feelings when he heard about the unauthorized thrill show out at Muroc. Although upset by the spectacular risks Yeager had taken, he could not help also feeling pride at what his hotshot young pilot had done. The memo he wrote reflected his ambivalence:

> I would personally like to have an explanation from you . . . as to your reasons for exceeding the authorized Mach number on this flight. . . . Please remember . . . the instructions I passed on to you personally here at Wright Field with respect to the value of the pilot and the plane to the Air Force. . . . The Air Force does not consider you or the plane expendable, so please approach higher speeds progressively and safely to the limit of your best judgement.[36]

Yeager drafted a response that seemed to satisfy Boyd. In it, he explained that the plane had flown so well that he did not think there would be a problem going above the target speed. Admitting he had been overly excited, he promised not to violate direct orders again.

With the chain of command firmly reestablished, the X-1 program continued. The next flights, however, would truly be into the unknown. Wind tunnels could only measure effects up to about .85 Mach, so there was no way of knowing what would happen next. It was "a very lonely feeling as we began to run out of data,"[37] confessed Walt Williams, one of the project's engineers. He knew that Yeager and the X-1 were about to enter unexplored territory.

7 Busting the Sound Barrier

Beginning in the fall of 1947, the men assigned to the X-1 project began a determined and ultimately successful assault on the sound barrier. Their quest turned out to be full of surprises, proving both easier and more difficult than they had imagined.

The X-1 could kill a pilot in a dozen ways, and the prospect of trouble at high speed and high altitude worried Yeager most. If the X-1 became uncontrollable, or if there were a fire or explosion, his only chance for survival would be to bail out. The cockpit door would pop off easily enough, but in an aircraft going more than 250 miles per hour, it would be nearly impossible to climb out against the pressure of the wind. Even if he did manage to get out of the cockpit, the wind would probably slam him back against the plane. Only six feet behind the cockpit door, the X-1's sharp little wing would probably slice him in two.

For most of that fall Yeager was able to keep such fears in the back of his mind as he and the X-1 crew eagerly approached the sound barrier. Ten years later, Walt Williams, then head of the NACA (National Advisory Committee for Aeronautics, the precursor of NASA) Flight Test Unit at Muroc, recalled the mood of the engineers and pilots:

We were enthusiastic, there is little question. The Air Force group—Yeager, Ridley—were very, very enthusiastic. We were just beginning to know each other, to work together. There had to be a balance between complete enthusiasm and the hard, cold facts. We knew and felt that if this program should fail the whole research airplane program would fail, the whole aeronautical effort would be set back.[38]

COLD WATER AND COLONEL BOYD

Because of his self-confidence and his impulsive nature, Yeager often did not see eye to eye with those who wanted to take things more slowly. Still worried that Yeager and Ridley might be too confident, Colonel Boyd had a long talk with them in his office at Wright Field in early October of 1947. It turned out to be an uncomfortable experience for the two young men. By then, the X-1 had reached .925 Mach. Boyd asked Ridley what he thought would happen in the final push to supersonic flight, and Ridley flatly replied that the plane would probably "just go eight-tenths faster."[39]

Yeager flies the X-1 in 1949. Sometimes he and his superiors disagreed on how quickly the X-1 program should have progressed.

Agreeing with his friend, Yeager added, "I don't really anticipate a great deal of difficulty, Colonel. It's been easy so far, easier than we all expected. Buffeting has been mild, and I've always had control of the airplane." Noting the sour look on Boyd's face, Yeager realized he might have overstated his case. "Well . . . most of the time,"[40] he added quickly.

Boyd then sternly reminded his two hotshot pilots that the X-1 had exhibited right-wing heaviness between .86 and .88 Mach, that it seemed to want to roll at .87 Mach, and that there had been increased buffeting above .86 Mach. Boyd wanted

Yeager and Ridley to seriously consider the possibility that they had just been lucky up to now—that things could get much worse as they reached the speed of sound. While Ridley might have been right about the lack of difficulties ahead, he could also have been wrong. This was no time for complacency.

Boyd then took Yeager and Ridley to lunch, but he was not through making his point. He introduced them to a group of generals by saying, "Couple of hot pilots here. Want to go back tonight and crash the sound barrier. No rudder, no elevator, buffeting getting severe at one speed, mild at the next. Nose up at Mach 0.87, nose down at .90. That airplane is likely to go in any direction, or all of them at once. But Captain Ridley and Captain Yeager here anticipate no difficulty in attaining Mach 1 over the weekend."[41]

AN INSOLUBLE PROBLEM?

On their return trip to Muroc, Ridley and Yeager were considerably less cocky and a little less likely to assume that everything would be all right. As if to underscore Colonel Boyd's point, an unexpected problem soon thereafter nearly ended the X-1 project. While flying at .94 Mach at forty thousand feet, Yeager experienced one of a test pilot's worst nightmares. When he pulled back on the control wheel, absolutely nothing happened. It felt to him as if the cables connected to the plane's elevator controls had snapped. (The elevator is the hinged flap on a plane's tail that tilts the plane's nose up or down.) Fighting panic, Yeager was relieved to discover that when the plane slowed, the elevator controls worked again.

Still, when he landed on the dry lakebed, he figured he had taken his last ride in the X-1. As he recalled some thirty years later, "It had been predicted that the X-1 would either pitch up or pitch down when I got in the region of the speed of sound. Now I had run out of ability to control the X-1."[42] It would be suicide to fly that fast with no control. A disheartened Yeager told Ridley that he could not see any way out of the dilemma.

After analyzing the data, the NACA engineers also became disheartened. At .94

Mach a shock wave from the plane's wings was hitting the hinge point of the elevator with such force that the controls were inoperable. It was a real crisis for the X-1 program. It appeared that the shape of the plane made supersonic flight impossible. Colonel Boyd flew out from Dayton to confer with Yeager, Ridley, and the engineers. Like Yeager, he could see no way past the problem.

RIDLEY'S BRAINSTORM

But then Ridley had an idea. The Bell engineers built in a design feature on the tail called the stabilizer system. A trim switch in the cockpit was connected to a small motor that could actually change the angle of the tail ever so slightly. Ridley wondered whether that small movement might be enough for a test pilot to regain control when the elevator did not work.

Because his idea was the only option they had, the engineers spent a day testing the trim switch on the ground. It worked well enough there, but no one knew if it would work at high speed. Perhaps the turbulent air would end up tearing off the X-1's tail. If that were the case, the result would be disastrous. Wanting to make sure Yeager understood the deadly risks involved, Colonel Boyd took him aside and told him that it would not be held against him if he decided against further flights.

Yeager explained that he trusted Ridley's judgment enough to take the X-1 up at least one more time. Still, the next flight was unusually tense. As Robert Cardenas, the B-29 pilot, recalled, the NACA engineers did not think Ridley knew what he was talking about:

> Chuck was aware, as I was, that the four Ph.D.'s on the ground thought we were going to kill Chuck and lose the airplane. I commented on this to Chuck. I said, "Chuck, if Ridley's right, you're going to be a hero. But if he's wrong, you're going to be dead. I don't mind making a decision but, on the other hand, it's your life." All Chuck said was, "If Jackie thinks I can do it, I'll do it. Somebody's got to do it, so I'll do it."[43]

When the test flight began, Yeager made tiny adjustments in pitch with the trim switch at .85 Mach. When things seemed to be working all right, he took the plane up to the speed where he had lost elevator control in the previous flight. To his great relief,

The X-1 featured a stabilizer on the tail that allowed Yeager to adjust the angle of the tail from the cockpit.

the new system of moving the tail gave him just enough control at .94 Mach to restore his confidence.

A Frosty Landing

The relief was short-lived, however. At forty-five thousand feet the cockpit window frosted over with a thick coating of ice. Unable to see, Yeager had to land the X-1 "blind" with the help of his chase pilot. Following radioed instructions and handling the controls as smoothly as possible, Yeager calmly brought the X-1 down with a perfect landing. With a touchdown speed of 190 miles per hour, anything less could have been disastrous.

When the data from the day's flight were analyzed, there was a surprise. Because of instrument error Yeager had flown a bit faster than he had thought. At approximately 658 miles per hour he had gone faster than any pilot ever, at least .997 Mach. With the X-1 program on the verge of reaching its goal, the next flight was scheduled for Tuesday, October 14. That weekend, Chuck took Glennis out for dinner. They got a babysitter and went to a place called Pancho Barne's Fly-Inn. The restaurant was also a dude ranch, so after dinner they decided to take a night ride in the desert. It was a decision Chuck would soon regret.

On the way back to the corral, they decided to race. Unfortunately, there was no moon that night. If there had been one, Chuck might have noticed that someone had shut the corral gate. Unable to stop in time, his horse barreled into the gate and Chuck was thrown for a spill, landing

hard on the desert floor. When he attempted to sit up, he noticed a sharp pain in his side. Glennis realized immediately that her husband had broken some ribs. She wanted him to go to the base hospital, but he refused. He knew the flight surgeon would have no choice but to ground him.

The Broomstick Scheme

On Monday he secretly went to a doctor off base who confirmed that he had two cracked ribs. Although he had the ribs taped up, the pain was so intense at times that it took his breath away. Still the thought of sitting out now after all he had gone through was too much to bear. (In truth, he was also afraid of what Colonel Boyd might say if he were grounded for falling off a horse.) Since the major control switches for the X-1 were within easy reach of the pilot, he figured he could still fly the plane. The hard part would be climbing down the ladder from the B-29 and squirming into the cockpit. But the most difficult problem of all would be finding a way to lock the cockpit door. Even when he was healthy, that took a lot of twisting and shoving to close. With cracked ribs, the task might be too painful to accomplish.

Yeager confided his problem to his friend Jack Ridley, and the two men devised a possible solution. Ridley sawed off a piece of a broomstick so that it could be slid through the door handle. With the broomstick secretly placed in the cockpit beforehand, Yeager just might gain enough leverage to push the door into the locked position without passing out from the pain.

On the morning of October 14, Glennis drove her husband to the base at six in the morning. She and Jack Ridley were the only ones who knew that he was going to try flying with broken ribs. She was not happy about it, but she trusted that Ridley would not let Yeager go if it was not safe. Before he said good-bye, Yeager made a mysterious request. He suggested that Glennis return to the base in time for the flight because something interesting might happen that day.

The NACA engineers advised Yeager that the plan for the day was to creep up toward .96 Mach, then back off unless absolutely certain that it was safe to go faster. At around eight in the morning the B-29, with the X-1 strapped underneath, took off to begin its spiraling climb to the drop altitude. When it reached an altitude of five thousand feet Yeager and Ridley climbed down the ladder to the X-1. It was a painfully slow process, but Yeager eventually worked his way into the cockpit. With Ridley on one side and Yeager with his broomstick

ON TOP OF THE WORLD

In the moments after he had broken the sound barrier, Chuck Yeager was alone in a way no other human being had ever been before. Tom Wolfe described the feeling in The Right Stuff.

"The X-1 had gone through the 'sonic wall' without so much as a bump. As the speed topped out at Mach 1.05, Yeager had the sensation of shooting straight through the top of the sky. The sky turned a deep purple and all at once the stars and the moon came out—and the sun shone at the same time. He had reached a layer of the upper atmosphere where the air was too thin to contain reflecting dust particles. He was simply looking out into space. As the X-1 nosed over at the top of the climb, Yeager now had seven minutes of . . . Pilot Heaven . . . ahead of him. He was going faster than any man in history, and it was almost silent up here, since he had exhausted his rocket fuel, and he was so high in such a vast space that there was no sensation of motion. He was master of the sky. His was a king's solitude, unique and inviolate, above the dome of the world. It would take him seven minutes to glide back down and land at Muroc. He spent the time doing victory rolls and wing-over-wing aerobatics while Rogers Lake and the Sierras spun around below."

on the other, the two managed to seal the cockpit door.

FLYING INTO HISTORY

After that it was a matter of going through his preflight checklist and then a few moments of tense waiting. At 10:26 A.M. at an altitude of twenty thousand feet, the X-1 dropped from the B-29 bomb bay into the bright California sunshine. For a few moments Yeager fought to get the plane's nose on an even keel. Then he fired all four rocket engines in rapid sequence. Under all six thousand pounds of thrust the little rocket plane shot forward, trailing a cone of fire.

Early in his ride, as the X-1 began its rapid climb, Yeager tested the stabilizer system to see whether it still gave him control. After passing thirty-five thousand feet in altitude he shut down two of the rocket engines to hold his speed at Mach 0.92. At forty-two thousand feet he reignited one of the shutdown engines. As he accelerated again, he experienced the same kind of buffeting that had occurred on previous flights. As before, elevator effectiveness decreased sharply at Mach .94, but pushing on to forty-two thousand feet, he received a pleasant surprise. Not only did the buffeting stop above Mach 0.96, but control of the elevators returned and the flight became much smoother—Jack Ridley's prediction had been correct.

With the X-1 apparently returning to its normal flying characteristics, Yeager felt no compulsion to cut the engines. At Mach .98 he felt a sudden increase in acceleration. The needle of his Machmeter fluctuated for a moment then jumped to 1.06. Later analysis of the data showed that he had hit Mach 1.07, or seven hundred miles per hour. Eight miles below on the desert floor, the men in the NACA tracking van reported hearing the distant rumble of thunder—the first sonic boom in history. Although Glennis did not hear the boom (the plane was too distant), she did see the flight, although she had little idea of its significance until later.

Meanwhile, Yeager could not resist hinting to his friend Ridley what had just happened. "Ridley!" he crowed. "Make another note. There's something wrong with this Machmeter. It's gone screwy!"[44]

Back in the B-29, Ridley played along, even though he could not mistake the triumphant tone in his buddy's voice. "If it is, we'll fix it," he replied. "Personally, I think you're seeing things."[45]

A SECRET CELEBRATION

When Yeager shut off the engines to end the powered portion of the flight, he noted a sharp bump as the plane decelerated past the sound barrier. During the glide back to Earth, it was so quiet inside the X-1 that the ticks of the cockpit clock were audible. "I was so high and remote, and the airplane was so very quiet that I might almost have been motionless," is how he described it.[46] In the silence, he had time to reflect on his mood, a curious mixture of elation and disappointment.

Somehow he had expected that breaking the sound barrier would be a little more difficult. In fact, the only way he had known for sure that he had gone beyond it was by looking at his instrument meter. He felt an emotional letdown. Later he would realize

An F/A-18 Hornet creates a cloud as it breaks the sound barrier in 1999. Yeager first broke the sound barrier in 1947.

that a letdown was inevitable since there was no actual sound barrier—just a barrier of knowledge.

Thankfully, there would be no frost-covered windows or blind landing on this flight. (The cockpit crew had discovered that coating the window with shampoo prevented the formation of ice.) Touchdown was routine, and after rolling approxi-

mately two and a half miles, the X-1 came to a stop. As usual, a fire truck was there to give a tired and stiff Yeager a ride back to the hangar.

He had just completed the first manned supersonic flight in history, and the word of the good news spread quickly within NACA, the air force, and the navy. Back on base, Yeager and Ridley called Colonel

Boyd to give him a personal account. By then Yeager was so tired that he just wanted to go home.

But the men who had worked on the X-1 project had other ideas. They planned a big party that night at Pancho's Fly-Inn—until Colonel Boyd called back to let them know that their achievement had been classified a military secret and word of it would not be given to the general public. So instead, a bunch of Yeager's friends and coworkers drove thirty miles across the desert to his house and celebrated there. After a few hours there they moved the party to Dick Frost's house. Later, Frost would write of the strangeness of that day: "It really was bizarre being forced to celebrate in secret the most historic flight of the age."[47]

Chapter

8 Pushing to Go Faster and Higher

Chuck Yeager's record-breaking assault on the sound barrier set the stage for the greatest advance in aviation since the Wright brothers. During the late 1940s and 1950s, a whole new supersonic air force was created. For the next six years Yeager was kept busier than ever, not only in highly experimental flight research programs but also in the evaluation of just about every aircraft being considered for the air force's operational fleet.

But exploring the flight characteristics of experimental aircraft in the unknown territory beyond Mach 1 was a deadly business that killed almost twenty of Yeager's fellow pilots. Meanwhile, although the news of his supersonic exploits made Yeager a reluctant public hero, the dangers he faced as a test pilot increased. Above Mach 1 in the X-1 a seemingly never-ending series of problems nearly cost Yeager his life. Although his steady nerves and superior piloting skills enabled him to survive each harrowing incident, the unending strain took its toll.

After more than thirty flights in the X-1 in thirteen months, Yeager would move on to test dozens of other experimental aircraft at Edwards Air Force Base (renamed in 1949 in honor of Glen Edwards, a young test pilot killed in 1948). Flying nearly every

day, as either a test pilot or a chase pilot, he maintained enthusiasm for his job while averaging a hundred flying hours a month for six years. "Flying experimental aircraft is addictive," noted Yeager's fellow test pilot, Bob Hoover. "Once it gets in the blood, there's no way to describe the rush of excitement that keeps a pilot going up day after day."[48]

DROPPING INTO DANGER

Following Yeager's record-breaking flight of October 14, 1947, the plan was to collect more valuable flight data as the plane flew even higher and faster. Fortunately for Yeager's broken ribs, he had two weeks to heal while the X-1's engine was overhauled. The rest was well timed because the next flight of the X-1 had some truly heart-stopping moments. As he dropped out of the bomb bay of the B-29, Yeager received a nasty shock—all of his electrical controls had gone dead and he was dropping like a stone toward the desert floor. Without electrical power, Yeager could not ignite the rocket engines or dump his explosive fuel (although he could still fly the plane manually as a glider).

Captain Yeager discusses his supersonic flights at a news conference in 1949. After breaking the sound barrier, Yeager went on to fly more than thirty test flights in the X-1.

But the X-1 was not designed to land with a full load of fuel. Its weight would surely collapse the landing gear, and then the first spark would set off a massive fireball. For a moment, it looked like his only chance for survival was to bail out and hope he could somehow avoid being sliced in two by the wing. Then he remembered that Bell engineer Dick Frost had installed a simple back-up system for use in case the electricity failed.

Frost had bought an inexpensive valve and connected it to a small bottle of nitrogen gas. In theory, by opening the valve using the pressure from the nitrogen, a pilot could manually dump his fuel. Yeager operated the valve, but because his radio was dead he could not ask his chase pilots to check and see whether it was really blowing out any fuel. As he neared the desert floor, he had no idea how much deadly fuel remained in the fuel tanks.

A Gooney Bird Goof

In the air force there has always been a good-natured rivalry between bomber pilots and fighter pilots. Often, while working at Edwards Air Force Base, Yeager and other fighter pilots would have occasion to hitch a ride on a bomber. On many such trips the bomber pilot was Bob Cardenas (the same man who had flown the B-29 that dropped the X-1 when Yeager broke the record). In Press On! *Yeager told about a diabolical practical joke he and his friends devised.*

"The Gooney Bird was a great plane to pull one of our favorite pranks. It didn't have seats—just a bench with lap belts where we passengers would sit—and beyond that the whole floor was open for hauling cargo. We knew that Cardenas was a good flier, very proud of his usually perfect landings. And so what we'd do was wait until he got the airplane set up and the landing gear down for his final approach. Then all of us fighter pilots would creep very slowly down to the back of the airplane. This moved the center of gravity, but since we'd made sure he had the flaps down first, Cardenas at this point wouldn't notice that anything was amiss.

We'd huddle in the tail together for a few moments, grinning at each other because we knew the best part was yet to come. Then, when Cardenas set himself up and trimmed the airplane up for a good landing, all of us would run like hell to the front. Now he's about fifty feet off the ground and the center of gravity has changed drastically. Invariably, the plane just heads down and *booms* against the runway a couple of times, making for one of the sorriest looking—and funniest—landings you've ever seen."

He also did not know whether his landing gear would stay locked down. (The light that normally told him the gear's status was also not working.) Not surprisingly, Yeager then made perhaps the longest, gentlest landing of his career, hovering inches above the desert floor for what seemed like an eternity. When the X-1 touched down and finally rolled to a stop, he breathed a huge sigh of relief.

But that was far from his last harrowing moment. In early November a crewman forgot to take the safety pin out of the mechanism that released the X-1 from the B-29 bomb bay. At the moment of the drop Yeager and the X-1 fell an inch or two and just hung there. When the B-29 was unable to shake the X-1 loose, Yeager had to climb back out of the cockpit and ascend the ladder, hoping that the X-1 would not drop in the middle of his exit.

He wasted no time scrambling back inside the B-29 and then had to endure more tense moments as they landed the bomber with the X-1 fastened precariously a few inches above the runway. Had it dropped any farther, the resulting explosion would have killed them all.

JINXED?

Maddeningly, the same thing happened on the very next flight. Although the safety pin was pulled this time, the X-1 just hung there, refusing to drop. Yeager was just unbuckling his safety harness to climb out again, when the X-1 lurched free of the bomber. At this point the X-1 was not moving fast enough for its wings to provide lift (pilots call it "stall speed"); Yeager had to dive the X-1 and hope to pick up enough speed to bring it back to level flight. He plunged five thousand feet before getting the plane under control and then ignited the rocket engines some twelve thousand feet lower than planned.

It was as if the X-1 program was jinxed. On another flight, after more problems with the release, Yeager was dropped under the stall speed again. By diving he got the plane back to level flight only to find that none of the rocket engines would ignite. Fortunately, he figured out an alternative way to ignite two of the engines, or it might well have been his last flight.

As harrowing as these moments were, they paled beside the kind of terror Yeager faced in January, February, and March of 1948. For an X-1 pilot sitting on all that volatile fuel, fire was always the worst fear. While flying at Mach 1.08 in late January,

Yeager was horrified to see smoke in the cockpit. He immediately cut his engines, dumped the remaining fuel, and landed, expecting to be blown to bits at any moment.

The next flight had to be aborted when the fire warning light came on. Despite a thorough check by the flight crew, the warning light came on again on the next flight and the cockpit filled with smoke. This kind of thing happened repeatedly for at least seven or eight flights.

SUPERSONIC NIGHTMARES

Yeager kept his doubts to himself, but his confidence in the X-1 was deeply shaken. At home, he started having nightmares about being burned alive. Glennis had to shake him awake at night. Once she even caught him trying to climb out of their bedroom window because it was shaped like an X-1 door.

Glennis had worries of her own in 1948. She was pregnant with their third child, and because her husband had flown higher and faster than anyone in history, there was considerable speculation in the press about what the world's first "supersonic baby" might look like. Sensational articles suggested that the child might be born deformed. Both parents were greatly relieved when their first daughter, Sharon, was born perfectly healthy.

Yeager was also relieved in the spring of 1948 when the Bell engineers finally discovered the source of the fire problem: During the engine overhaul a gasket had been installed improperly. Still, after a couple more uneventful flights, Yeager had yet

Yeager and his family pose for a photograph in 1949. Both Yeager and his wife, Glennis, were relieved when their "supersonic" daughter, Sharon (right, on mother's lap), was born healthy.

another hair-raising moment. When a faulty switch prevented him from igniting his rocket engines, he managed to dump his fuel and glide safely back to Earth. It was then that Colonel Boyd decided his star pilot deserved a break from the relentless pressure.

For the next few months, someone else would fly the X-1. Yeager, meanwhile, flew as chase pilot on X-1 flights and piloted other experimental craft as needed. As a chase pilot, Yeager was considered the absolute best. With his sharp eyes and intimate knowledge of the X-1's mechanical systems, he could spot and diagnose trouble instantly and save precious seconds when a man's life was at stake.

Bill Bridgeman, a former navy fighter pilot, gave thanks for Yeager's mechanical abilities and chase pilot skills on more than one occasion. Bridgeman flew the Douglas Skyrocket, the navy's version of the X-1 program. Since the Skyrocket had an engine and flight characteristics similar to those of the X-1, Yeager was often asked to fly chase.

SOME LIFESAVING ADVICE

One day Bridgeman's fire warning light came on as black smoke poured out of his engine. He was afraid to dump his fuel because he thought the engine fire might ignite it and blow everything up. Flying alongside, Yeager calmly told him to ease back on the throttle. When he did, the smoke thinned. Yeager knew that this indicated the fire was inside the jet engine and not inside the rocket chambers. Bridgeman survived after Yeager instructed him to turn off the engine and hit the fire extinguisher, then dump his fuel, and glide back down to the desert floor.

That dry desert lakebed was the test pilot's friend. Neither Yeager nor Bridgeman would have disagreed with Bud Anderson's assessment:

> The psychological lift that lakebed gives you is simply tremendous. Lose an engine and it's no big deal. If you lose one at Wright-Patterson, that's a big deal, getting it back on the runway. . . . But at Edwards, out over the desert, there are miles of flat surface below you. You can make big mistakes, and put the plane down almost anywhere. . . . Psychologically, it's almost like having a parachute versus not having one.[49]

In the late 1940s both the navy and the brand new air force tested their planes on the lakebed at Edwards. The rivalry between the two services was intense—so in-

tense that it lured Yeager back into the X-1. The navy claimed that the X-1 was just a gimmick and that its Douglas D-558-I Skystreak was a superior plane because it could take off from the ground.

SHOWING UP THE NAVY

That really annoyed Yeager. He wondered whether it would be possible to try a ground takeoff with the X-1 to take the steam out of the navy's publicity campaign. After getting an okay from the secretary of the air force, he set to work to do just that.

Working with his friend Jack Ridley, Yeager devised a flight plan that called for the X-1 to be filled with half a tank of fuel for the ground takeoff. (Any more fuel than that and their landing gear would collapse.) On the morning of January 5, 1949, Yeager strapped himself into the X-1 for what may have been the most exhilarating minute and a half any airplane pilot has ever experienced.

"There was no ride ever in the world like that one!"[50] he said later. Igniting the rocket, he streaked down the runway, jumped into the air at about two hundred miles per hour, raised the nose sharply, and rode a tail of flame into the stratosphere. Eighty seconds later, he was at twenty-three thousand feet and flying at Mach 1.03.

The next day the navy was scheduled to fly its new rocket-powered model of the Skystreak, but just as he had hoped, Yeager's spectacular takeoff stole the spotlight. Although his daredevil feat made him a hero to many in the air force, the X-1's useful life was almost at an end. A few months later it was flown to Washington to be permanently installed in the Smithsonian Institution as a pioneering aircraft.

RIVALRY TO GO FASTER AND HIGHER

The rivalry between the services added unanticipated complications to Yeager's life. In the years to come the public would make much of the competition between the air force, navy, and NACA to go fastest and highest. Former navy pilot Scott Crossfield, who arrived at Edwards in 1950 as a NACA X-15 test pilot, gained a reputation as Yeager's main competitor in a rivalry that took on a legendary character.

Not long after Yeager broke the sound barrier, word leaked to the public about what he had done. Soon after, the air force

Yeager showed up the U.S. Navy by proving the X-1 could take off from the ground.

An Unbreakable Record

In his book, Supersonic Flight, *Richard Hallion revealed how Yeager's difficulties and incredible recovery on December 12, 1953, led to the abandonment of further X-1 flights above Mach 2.*

"As the X-1A touched down in a plume of dust, Yeager summed up his feeling about the flight. 'You know,' he radioed, 'if I'd had an ejection seat, you wouldn't still see me in this thing.' The young pilot got out of the rocket plane, having completed one of the wildest, roughest, yet shortest flights in aviation history. For the flight, Yeager later received the Harmon Trophy. On the flight, NACA radar tracking records indicated the plane attained a peak speed of 1,612 mph at 74,200 feet. . . . The plane's difficulties led to immediate recognition that airplanes flying beyond Mach 2.3 would require much larger vertical and horizontal stabilizer surfaces to retain adequate stability at high Mach numbers.

. . . Yeager's Mach 2.44 flight represented the highwater mark of the entire X-1 program. No X-1 airplane ever equaled or exceeded this speed mark."

realized that his growing fame could be useful. Besides his test pilot duties, he was ordered to fly around the country, giving speeches and making public appearances. The last thing Yeager wanted to do was to stand up and give a speech in front of a crowd. He hated wearing a tie and was self-conscious about his West Virginia twang and lack of education.

He protested but was told he had no choice. Soon he was making fifteen to twenty appearances per month. Although he felt awkward at first, audiences loved his direct style of speaking. Magazines and newspapers praised his achievements, and he even appeared on the cover of *Time* magazine. All that publicity (much of it embroidered or inaccurate) made Yeager uncomfortable. He had enough to worry about just doing his job.

That he survived those first years at Edwards was a minor miracle. When something goes wrong at supersonic speed a pilot often has only a couple of seconds to take corrective action. Yet Yeager was kept busy flying so many different kinds of planes—as many as twenty-seven models in a single month—that he did not have time to carefully study the emergency systems that could save his life. Often it was only his uncanny instincts that kept him out of trouble.

Solving a Deadly Mystery

Those same instincts also saved other lives. Not long after three pilots died mysteriously while doing rolls in their F-86 Sabre jets, Yeager was flying over the Sierras in his F-86. A friend's home was on a mountain lake nearby, so he decided to buzz the house and do a slow roll. In the middle of that roll, the F-86's ailerons (the flaps that tilt a plane's wings) locked up. It was a scary moment, flying upside down only 150 feet above the ground, but Yeager did not panic. When he eased up on the throttle and pushed the nose upward, the ailerons unlocked and he was able to return to level flight.

Puzzled, Yeager took his plane up to a safer altitude and tried the roll again and again. Each time the ailerons would lock, then unlock when he eased up. His mechanical intuition told him that somehow the wings were bending under stress and interfering with the ailerons. When he reached the ground he called Colonel Boyd and told him he thought he knew how those other F-86 pilots had died, although he did not know why.

When investigators disassembled the wings of his plane they discovered a bolt installed incorrectly. The problem was traced back to a line worker at the aircraft assembly plant who had been putting the bolt in upside down for months. His mistake would undoubtedly have killed many more pilots had Yeager not discovered the problem on the fly.

Unfortunately, he would soon encounter a flight emergency beyond anyone's capabilities. Early in 1953, Bell Aircraft's latest experimental plane, the X-1A, arrived at Edwards. A longer, more powerful plane than the X-1, it had a bubble canopy that gave the pilot better vision. It was also designed to fly twenty or thirty thousand feet higher than the X-1 at speeds greater than Mach 2.

A Difficult New Challenge

As with the X-1, Bell had hired a civilian test pilot, but when he was killed testing another Bell plane Yeager was given the assignment. Ordinarily, he would have been enthusiastic about starting a new program with a hot new plane. That was not the case this time. Glennis was very sick and the doctors could not find a reason for her illness. Pregnant with their fourth child, she had a fever and aching joints that kept her bedridden for months.

For the first time Yeager, now a major, realized how much he had relied on his wife to run things while he was flying. Preoccupied with her health, he was unable to give his full attention to the X-1A. Fortunately, the plane was not ready to fly until November of 1953. By then, Glennis had given birth to their daughter Susie, soon after which her mysterious sickness disappeared.

The first three flights in the X-1A went well, although Yeager was uneasy about the complete lack of an ejection seat (the pilot was simply locked inside the canopy). Three weeks earlier a NACA Skyrocket had gone to Mach 2, so for his fourth flight on December 12 he intended to take the record back for the air force.

All went according to plan at first. At 74,200 feet he hit Mach 2.44, a speed of

An A-7 Corsair aircraft flies upside down, while another flies upright. Flying upside down in an F-86, Yeager discovered the cause of death of so many pilots of this aircraft.

1,612 miles per hour. It was a new speed record and the fastest any straight-winged aircraft would ever fly. But only ten seconds after leveling off, the plane began a slow roll to the left. When Yeager corrected for it, the X-1A rolled violently to the right and began tumbling wildly.

The technical name for this is "going divergent on all three axes," but what it really means is that a plane is no longer flying. As the X-1A twisted, tumbled, and rolled

crazily across the sky, Yeager was too busy fighting for his life to communicate with anyone.

THE CLOSEST CALL

Meanwhile, the chase plane pilots and ground trackers listened in vain for some word from him on the radio. Subjected to as much as eleven times the normal force of gravity, he was slammed around inside the cockpit with such violence that his helmet cracked the canopy. Battered and bruised, he came close to losing consciousness.

Spinning like a badly thrown Frisbee, his plane dropped more than nine and a half miles in fifty-one seconds. Complicating manners greatly, the cold air streaming in through the cracked cockpit frosted over the faceplate on his pressure suit. Unable to see and close to losing consciousness, Yeager was certain he was going to die.

At one point he was thrown against the control stick and his helmet somehow hooked onto it; struggling to free himself, Yeager caught glimpses of light and dark as the plane spun toward then away from the sun. Somehow, amid all the chaos, he recalled that the stabilizer switch was set in "leading edge full down" position. Although unable to see he knew exactly where that switch was.

Groping for it, he made an adjustment, then located a switch for the heat. What he saw when his faceplate cleared was not encouraging. He was spinning into the Sierras and had less than a minute before impact. Then his flying instincts took over. By operating the controls to coincide with the movements of the spin he gradually re-gained some control of the X-1A. Finally, at thirty thousand feet the plane flipped into a normal spin. Yeager now had some hope—he knew how to get out of a normal spin.

At twenty-five thousand feet, the X-1A escaped from the spin and began flying again. In a breathless, desperate voice Yeager came back on the radio: "I'm down to 25,000 over Tehachapi. . . . Don't know whether I can make it back to the base or not." When asked for clarification on where he was, he could only gasp, "I can't say much more. I gotta save myself."[51]

He was so dazed he did not know whether he could land, and, of course, he did not know whether the plane had been damaged. Thankfully, his head began to clear at 5,000 feet, and he began to think that he might survive after all. At 270 miles per hour he got the X-1A lined up for a landing. Although he came in uncharacteristically hard with a thump and a cloud of dust, it was the sweetest landing he ever made.

Safe on the ground, he began thinking seriously about getting out of the test pilot business. Pilots who survived for any length of time did so on skill and luck. His skills had not diminished, but by December 1953 he had a feeling that his luck had about run out.

Chapter

9 No Slowing Down

After completing a top-secret mission early in 1954—perhaps his most dangerous assignment ever—Chuck Yeager left test piloting to begin a new and satisfying phase of his life. During the rest of his air force career, and through a retirement that lasted into the twenty-first century, he continued making contributions to aviation and to his country. Fittingly, for a man who had broken the sound barrier, he also helped train the pilots and astronauts who would explore the next great aviation frontier—space.

Through it all, Chuck Yeager continued to fly every chance he got. Despite his love of flying, he found little to enjoy about the mission he found himself on in February of 1954. It all began when a North Korean pilot defected to South Korea in his MiG 15 fighter plane. Only months before, these Russian-built fighters had been in combat against American Sabre jets in the Korean War. Although a truce had been signed in 1953, fighting could break out again at any moment.

Getting hold of an intact enemy fighter was a real intelligence bonanza, but someone would be needed to test the plane's capabilities quickly and quietly. That was why Yeager got a call from Albert Boyd, who had

been promoted to general by then. Yeager and another test pilot, along with Boyd, flew to Okinawa, where they tested the plane in secret. The mission was to find out what the MiG 15 could and could not do.

It was a risky business since it meant intentionally taking an unfamiliar plane to the very limit of its abilities. To make matters more difficult, the entire week that Yeager was in Okinawa, a tropical storm swept the island. Despite the rain and poor visibility, Yeager flew the MiG 15 higher and faster than any Russian pilot had ever dared.

PUSHING THE BOUNDARIES

The MiG 15 was a difficult and tricky airplane to fly—one that had even killed pilots who were familiar with it. Yet, despite unfamiliar gauges based on the metric system and horrible weather, Yeager pushed the aircraft beyond what any sane pilot would have attempted. The worst moment was probably when he set out to prove whether the MiG 15 was actually supersonic. Some of the pilots who had been in dogfights against it believed it was, but no one knew for sure. The truth would be extremely

A soldier stands guard over a MiG 15 in 1954. Yeager was sent to South Korea to test the plane.

valuable information. To Yeager and Boyd this seemed doubtful, since the Russians had built in an automatic speed brake at .94 Mach. They decided to find out for sure—even though they suspected the air brakes were there for good reason. Because of the risks, Boyd gave Yeager the option of backing away from the job, but Yeager declined—even though he thought it likely he would have to use the ejection seat.

From a height of fifty thousand feet, Yeager put the MiG into a screaming dive to see just how fast he could get the unfamiliar aircraft to go. Above Mach .94 the plane shuddered and shook, and he lost elevator and aileron control. Plunging toward the ground at close to the speed of sound, Yeager was no longer flying the plane. Thankfully, in the denser air at sixteen thousand feet he began to feel some control effect. A

ANOTHER DAY AT THE OFFICE

In The Quest for Mach One, *published on the fiftieth anniversary of the breaking of the sound barrier, aviation writer Jeff Ethell noted how Chuck Yeager has remained unimpressed by his celebrity.*

"In the same way the quarterback's name on a championship team will always be remembered more than anyone else's, the name Chuck Yeager will always be associated first and foremost with the breaking of the sound barrier. He was the man at the controls of the X-1 as it broke through the sonic wall. He is also the man who will tell you that the X-1 program was a team effort, and that the glory that has come his way is shared by everyone associated with the project. Here at the reminiscing stage, fifty years from the golden moment, you might expect Yeager to be sentimental about it. You would be wrong. Yeager has spent the last fifty years refusing to act like a big hero. He is matter-of-fact about his accomplishments. In his view there was a job to be done, the engineers and Jackie Ridley said it could be done, he was being paid by the Air Force to fly, somebody had do it—so he did it. Even the exact moment of the sonic breach was taken in stride. . . . Yeager said to Jackie Ridley over the radio, 'We have problems. This ol' Mach meter is plumb off the scale.' No fireworks, no bands playing. Yeager, after landing the X-1 on the Rogers Dry Lake, was towed back to Operations standing on the X-1's wing. He was happy, . . . but it was just another day at the office."

Colonel Yeager visits with actor James Stewart.

few thousand feet lower, he pulled out of the dive—right in the middle of a storm cloud. He then made a difficult landing in the midst of a blinding rainstorm. He had taken the MiG 15 up to .98 Mach, undoubtedly faster than any Russian had ever flown it. And the information he had provided proved that, in most respects, the Sabre jets were superior aircraft.

General Cannon, then head of the air force in the Pacific, was astonished at how much Yeager had accomplished in such lousy weather. "General," Boyd told him, "just be thankful that the enemy doesn't have a test pilot with the skills of Major Yeager. Because of him, we now know more about the plane than the Russians do."[52]

A HERO'S REWARD

Boyd considered Yeager the best pilot he had ever seen. On their flight home, he asked Yeager what he would like to do after test piloting. When Yeager expressed interest in being in a fighter squadron again, Boyd said he would see what he could do. A few weeks later, Yeager was offered command of the 417th Fighter Squadron in Germany. He wasted little time in accepting the offer—after seven years in the high California desert, Glennis was ready to move. When Yeager told her about their new assignment, she was as happy as he had ever seen her.

Soon after he arrived at the base in Hahn, Germany, Yeager was promoted to lieutenant colonel. At age thirty-one he was already a legend in the air force. At first the younger pilots could not wait to challenge their new commander in mock dogfights.

But once he had beaten them all with ease, he earned their lasting respect. During three years in Europe, Yeager received high marks for his leadership abilities. His squadron was the best-performing squadron in the wing and won numerous awards. Glennis and the kids loved living in Europe and were sorry when their tour of duty ended in September 1957. Glennis was even sorrier when she learned where they would be going next.

Yeager had accepted command of the First Fighter Squadron, flying new supersonic F-100 Super Sabres, at George Air Force Base, California, only fifty miles from Edwards; once again, the Yeager family was back in the desert. Yeager, however, was excited about the assignment. During the early 1950s he had tested the prototypes of the Super Sabres. Now he would help these new aircraft became part of the air force. His squadron at George, an elite group of superb pilots, was deployed all over the world on short notice. Yeager claimed they were the best bunch he had ever flown with. He also claimed that the two years he spent at George were the most fun he had had as a squadron commander.

IN TROUBLE AGAIN

Unfortunately, on a deployment to a base in Italy in the winter of 1959, he had a little too much fun. A squadron party got out of hand and led to some damage to the base officers' club. Athough Yeager paid for the damage out of his own pocket, the base commander wanted him court-martialed. Yeager was terrified when he received a curt note from the Tactical Air Command headquarters. He was told to return to the States and report directly to General Frank Everest. The flight back across the Atlantic was one of the longest he had ever made. The air force was the only job he had ever had, and the possibility of being forced out in disgrace was almost more than he could bear to think about.

But after chewing Yeager out for the party, Everest surprised him by commending him for doing a good job with his squadron. Everest then revealed that Yeager had been pulled out of Italy for his own good. Government property had been damaged. If charges had been filed and he had been found responsible, his career would be over. Everest explained that Yeager's superiors had decided to send

Yeager tests an NF-760. He was always eager to be among the first to fly new planes.

him to the Air War College in Montgomery, Alabama, instead.

Going to school for ten months would not be as enjoyable as flying the latest supersonic fighter planes, but Yeager was just grateful that his career had not been ruined. While at the Air War College, he received a promotion to colonel. After his graduation in the summer of 1961, he returned to Edwards to head the new Aerospace Research Pilot School, as the USAF Test Pilot School was then designated. The mission of the school was to train the first generation of military astronauts. During the five years that Yeager was there the school provided the National Air and Space Administration (NASA) with nearly half of its astronauts, as well as training many of those who, in years to come, would fly the space shuttle.

ANOTHER NARROW ESCAPE

Yeager's post at Edwards was his first true nonflying job. He was surprised by how much he enjoyed it, but he did not give up flying, or danger, entirely. In 1963 the school received three rocket-powered F-104 Starfighters. They were going to be used to provide future astronauts training in zero gravity at high altitude. But first Yeager wanted to check the planes out and, while he was at it, set a new altitude record. On the morning of December 12, 1963, he took an F-104 up to 108,000 feet, nearly twenty-one miles above the earth.

That afternoon he went up again to double check the F-104's flight characteristics. At 104,000 feet the plane's nose pitched up. When Yeager tried controlling the pitch,

nothing happened. Suddenly the plane went into a flat spin. Revolving slowly like a record on a turntable, the F-104 would not respond to any maneuver Yeager tried. It fell almost twenty miles before he conceded failure and bailed out. He was the first pilot to eject while wearing the full pressure suit needed for high-altitude flights. He also came frighteningly close to being the first to die. When a rocket charge blasted Yeager and his seat out of the plane, the still-burning seat became tangled with his parachute. Then it smashed into his facemask, knocking out the faceplate.

As pure oxygen poured out of the suit, it was if a blowtorch had been lit. Yeager's face and head were engulfed in flames. Unable to see and choking on the smoke, he instinctively brushed at the smoke with his free hand. When it, too, caught fire, he was sure he was going to die. Finally, he thought to snap his visor open, automatically shutting off the oxygen supply. A few seconds later, he hit the ground hard, smoke and fire still pouring out of his helmet.

He wrestled the helmet off with his bare hands and then waited for help. With his face and hand badly charred, he was not a pretty sight. He had come down near a highway, and the first motorist who stopped to help was so sickened he had to turn away. Finally, a helicopter arrived to take Yeager back to the base hospital. Yeager's recovery from severe burns was miraculous, but the extensive skin grafts he had to endure to minimize disfigurement inflicted the worst pain he had ever known. Still, when the doctors were finally through with him, a few scars on his neck and the missing tips of two fingers were the only evidence of the accident.

THE FLYING GENERAL

Colonel Yeager continued working with future military astronauts and pilots until 1966, when NASA took over the training of astronauts. Later that year, he took command of the 405th Fighter Wing at Clark Air Base in the Philippines. As wing commander, he was responsible for the performance and morale of five thousand men scattered all across Southeast

---

IT HAD TO BE FUN

In Press On!, *Yeager's lifelong friend, Bud Anderson, talked about the flip side of Yeager's devotion to duty.*

"His attitude has always been: 'If something's not fun, why do it?' What he does, really, is manage to *make* fun from just about any situation he encounters. I went to our Fighter Group reunion not long ago, and after all these years, I saw something there that summed up Chuck Yeager pretty neatly. There was this former Red Cross girl who was passing around a scrapbook that had pictures of us in wartime England. One in particular caught my eye because it was of a bunch of pilots standing on a beach amidst those dragon-toothed anti-invasion devices they had embedded along the shore. Everyone was in uniform except for one guy. There, lying out in the sand in front of the others—and wearing swimming trunks and a big smile—was my friend Yeager. Now, it would never have occurred to me, in the middle of the daily life-and-death struggle of a major war, to go swimming. But apparently, it had occurred to Chuck, and he'd even managed somehow to get himself a pair of trunks.

So, while 'fun' may be altogether too limited a word to define the many different kinds of feelings Chuck gets from his all-out approach to living—all the way from the tough-won serenity of the Sierras to the high of aerial combat—it is the word he would use in his thinking; it's how he'd define whether or not a thing was worth doing, or a person worth knowing."

Asia. With his fighters and bombers at bases in the Philippines, Vietnam, Thailand, and Taiwan, Yeager had to do a lot of flying just to check on them. (He visited each base every ten days or so.) During his two years at Clark, he also managed to fit in 127 combat missions over South Vietnam.

After a stint as commander of the Fourth Tactical Fighter Wing at Seymour Johnson Air Force Base in North Carolina, he was named vice commander of the Seventh Air Force in Ramstein, Germany. Shortly before his arrival there in the summer of 1969, he received the stunning news that he was to be promoted to brigadier general. He had always assumed that his lack of formal education precluded him from ever rising higher than colonel. He had never dreamed that an uneducated "hillbilly" who had not gone to college and had begun his military career as a lowly private would ever be addressed as "General Yeager." It was a sweet moment, made all the sweeter by the fact that he and Glennis would be returning to Germany.

One Last Special Mission

The Yeagers enjoyed their stay at Ramstein, but the air force had another big surprise in store. Around Christmas of 1970, air force headquarters notified Yeager that he was being sent on a special mission to Pakistan. As U.S. defense representative to Pakistan, his assignment was to train and advise the Pakistani air force. Military regulations normally forbade generals from flying their own planes, but the unusual nature of this job meant he could pilot a plane again.

When the Pakistan assignment ended after almost two years the Yeagers returned to the United States—and California—one last time. In 1973, Yeager's new assignment at Norton Air Force Base was as director of the air force Safety and Inspection Center. His work involved lots of travel, and he successfully lobbied the Pentagon to be allowed to fly on the job. He was delighted to be the only general in the air force certified to pilot an airplane.

Honors and Awards

On March 1, 1975, at the age of fifty-two, Yeager retired from the military, just after his induction into the Aviation Hall of Fame in Dayton, Ohio. A year later Congress awarded him the Congressional Medal of Honor for his contributions to aviation. He is the only person ever awarded this honor in peacetime.

Indeed, Yeager has received every major award in the field of aviation, including the Collier Trophy for achievement in aviation development; the Harmon International Trophy, awarded to the world's outstanding aviators; and the Federation Aeronautique International Gold Medal. Along with the medal of honor, he is the recipient of the Presidential Medal of Freedom (1985), the second of America's two highest civilian honors. His military decorations include the Distinguished Flying Cross with two oak leaf clusters, the Distinguished Service Medal, and the Legion of Merit.

In the years since his retirement, Yeager has remained actively involved with aviation. He gives speeches all over the world and has acted as an adviser for aviation

President Reagan presents the Presidential Medal of Freedom to Yeager in 1985. Yeager has been awarded numerous medals and honors throughout his career.

films and documentaries. Yeager was memorably portrayed by actor Sam Shepard in the 1983 feature film *The Right Stuff,* based on Tom Wolfe's best-selling book about the first astronauts. Yeager's exploits were featured prominently in the book, which helped introduce him to a whole new generation. Yeager himself appeared in the film in a cameo role; in a humorous twist, he played the bartender who serves the rowdy flyboys who spend their off-duty hours at Pancho's.

A SUPERSONIC RETIREE

As always, Yeager has continued flying. Both NASA and the air force signed him on as a consultant to fly the newest planes being tested at Edwards Air Force Base. "I'm very fortunate because I get to work on current programs, and I'm probably the only guy in the world who's been allowed to do

Yeager retired from the military in 1975 with the rank of brigadier general.

that," Yeager noted with satisfaction in 1997. "I have never quit or fallen behind. If I did, I'd probably never catch up."[53]

Always interested in new challenges, he took up hang gliding and flew ultralight airplanes in his retirement. He also frequently indulged his passion for hunting and fishing in hard-to-reach wilderness areas all over the world. His retirement, however, has had its share of sorrow. In 1990 Glennis Yeager died of cancer. Seven years later Yeager fell from a twelve-foot ladder, cracking ribs, separating a shoulder, and fracturing his collarbone. "He had complications during recovery," noted his friend, Bud Anderson, "and twice while in intensive care they put the electric paddles to his chest to restore a regular heartbeat."[54]

Yet, only two months later, he was flying a Mustang in an air show with Anderson. Then, on October 14, 1997, exactly fifty years after he shattered the sound barrier in the X-1, Yeager marked the anniversary by flying above Mach 1 in an F-15 fighter. Anderson tells what happened afterward:

> Chuck announced that he was retiring from his test-pilot consultant job at Edwards, a role that had allowed him to fly anything in the arsenal. He was going out on top after fifty-five years of flying high-performance aircraft. At seventy-five, he still has a Class II FAA medical certificate with no limitations.

Of course, he'll still fly the Mustang. Light planes, too. . . . His injuries still nagged him in June, but that didn't stop him from going on our annual backpacking trip. Only difference was, we did it on horseback! Chuck is still Chuck. Bigger than life.[55]

THE SOUND OF A BARRIER BUSTER

Five years later, on October 26, 2002, Yeager opened an air show at Edwards Air Force Base by flying an F-15 Eagle at 1.45 Mach, almost one and a half times the speed of sound. Although, at nearly eighty years of age, he claimed this would be his last supersonic flight, he managed to excite the crowd in much the same way he had thrilled his comrades on the X-1 project some fifty-five years earlier. "I was standing in the hangar when General Yeager flew by," said sixteen-year-old Jennifer Thompson of Martinez, California. "He shook the whole hangar—it was really cool."[56]

Now in his seventh decade of flying, Yeager has spent more than fourteen thousand hours in more than 330 different types and models of military aircraft. But more than the amount of time he has spent in the

air or his piloting skill makes Yeager unique—his philosophy too remains extraordinary: "I wasn't a deep sophisticated person, but I lived by a basic principle: I did only what I enjoyed. I wouldn't let anyone derail me by promises of power or money into doing things that weren't interesting to me."[57]

In a life spent almost exclusively pursuing projects that interested him, Chuck Yeager has been a pioneer who has courageously flown into dangerous and uncharted territory and then on to the edge of space itself. For these achievements, he richly deserves mention alongside aviation heroes like the Wright brothers and Charles Lindbergh.

The citation accompanying his Congressional Medal of Honor celebrates his record-breaking flight of October 14, 1947; it also sums up his entire career:

He dispelled for all time the mythical "sound barrier" and set the stage for unprecedented aviation advancement. Through his selfless dedication to duty and his heroic challenge of the unknown, General Yeager performed inestimable service to the Nation far above and beyond the call of duty and brought great credit upon himself and the United States of America.[58]

Notes

Introduction: A Supersonic Pioneer

1. Quoted in General Chuck Yeager and Leo Janos, *Yeager: An Autobiography*. New York: Bantam Books, 1985, p. 239.
2. Yeager and Janos, *Yeager*, p. 239.

Chapter 1: The Hillbilly from Hamlin

3. General Chuck Yeager and Charles Leerhsen, *Press On! Further Adventures in the Good Life*. New York: Bantam Books, 1988, pp. 161–62.
4. Yeager and Leerhsen, *Press On!*, p. 1.
5. Yeager and Leershen, *Press On!*, pp. 66–67.
6. Yeager and Janos, *Yeager*, p. 10.

Chapter 2: A Hunter Takes Wing

7. Quoted in Carl von Wodtke and Jon Guttman, "Chuck Yeager in Combat," *Aviation History*, May 1998, p. 22.
8. von Wodtke and Guttman, "Chuck Yeager in Combat," p. 22.
9. Yeager and Janos, *Yeager*, pp. 21–22.
10. Yeager and Janos, *Yeager*, p. 25.

Chapter 3: Downed but Not Out: Behind Enemy Lines

11. Quoted in Clarence E. "Bud" Anderson, *To Fly and Fight: Memoirs of a Triple Ace*. Pacifica, CA: Pacifica Military History, 1990, p. 87.
12. Yeager and Janos, *Yeager*, p. 63.
13. Quoted in von Wodtke and Guttman, "Chuck Yeager in Combat," p. 23.
14. Quoted in Yeager and Janos, *Yeager*, p. 37.
15. Quoted in Yeager and Janos, *Yeager*, p. 39.

Chapter 4: The College of Life and Death: World War II Air Combat

16. Quoted in von Wodtke and Guttman, "Chuck Yeager in Combat," p. 24.

17. von Wodtke and Guttman, "Chuck Yeager in Combat," p. 25.
18. von Wodtke and Guttman, "Chuck Yeager in Combat," p. 25.
19. Anderson, *To Fly and Fight*, p. 165.
20. Yeager and Janos, *Yeager*, p. 88.

Chapter 5: Hog Heaven

21. Anderson, *To Fly and Fight*, p. 176.
22. Yeager and Janos, *Yeager*, p. 104.
23. Quoted in R.A. "Bob" Hoover, *Forever Flying*. New York: Pocket Books, 1996, p. 94.
24. Hoover, *Forever Flying*, p. 95.

Chapter 6: Riding the Bullet: The X-1

25. Hoover, *Forever Flying*, p. 101.
26. Quoted in Yeager and Janos, *Yeager*, p. 120.
27. Quoted in Chuck Yeager, Bob Cardenas, Bob Hoover, Jack Russell, and James Young, *The Quest for Mach One*. New York: Penguin Studio, p. 135.
28. Hoover, *Forever Flying*, p. 113.
29. Yeager and Janos, *Yeager*, p. 123.
30. Quoted in Richard P. Hallion, *Test Pilots: The Frontiersmen of Flight*. Washington, DC: Smithsonian Institution Press, 1991, p. 199.
31. Quoted in Louis Rotundo, *Into the Unknown: The X-1 Story*. Washington, DC: Smithsonian Institution Press, 1994, p. 253.
32. Quoted in William R. Lundgren, *Across the High Frontier: The Story of a Test Pilot*. New York: William Morrow, 1955, p. 202.
33. Lundgren, *Across the High Frontier*, p. 202.
34. Quoted in Rotundo, *Into the Unknown*, p. 254.
35. Quoted in Rotundo, *Into the Unknown*, p. 255.

36. Quoted in Rotundo, *Into the Unknown*, p. 255.

37. Quoted in Richard P. Hallion, *Designers and Test Pilots.* Alexandria, VA: Time-Life Books, 1983, p. 119.

Chapter 7: Busting the Sound Barrier

38. Quoted in Richard P. Hallion, *Supersonic Flight: Breaking the Sound Barrier and Beyond.* New York: Macmillan, 1972, p. 105.

39. Quoted in Rotundo, *Into the Unknown*, p. 267.

40. Quoted in Rotundo, *Into the Unknown*, p. 267.

41. Quoted in Rotundo, *Into the Unknown*, p. 268.

42. Hallion, *Test Pilots*, p. 199.

43. Yeager, Cardenas, Hoover, Russell, and Young, *The Quest for Mach One*, p. 99.

44. Quoted in Lundgren, *Across the High Frontier*, p. 241.

45. Quoted in Lundgren, *Across the High Frontier*, p. 241.

46. Quoted in Suzanne Levert, *The Doubleday Book of Famous Americans.* Garden City, NY: Doubleday, 1989, p. 303.

47. Quoted in Yeager and Janos, *Yeager*, p. 167.

Chapter 8: Pushing to Go Faster and Higher

48. Hoover, *Forever Flying*, p. 157.

49. Anderson, *To Fly and Fight*, p. 207.

50. Yeager and Janos, *Yeager*, p. 197.

51. Transcript of cockpit audio from December 12, 1953, at "Chuck Yeager: Flying the X-1A," 2002. www.chuckyeager.com.

Chapter 9: No Slowing Down

52. Quoted in Yeager and Janos, *Yeager*, p. 263.

53. Quoted in Bryan Ethier, "Breaking the Sound Barrier," *American History*, September/October 1997, p. 24.

54. Anderson, *To Fly and Fight*, p. 305.

55. Anderson, *To Fly and Fight*, p. 305.

56. From "Yeager Breaks the Barrier One Last Time," www.cnn.com.

57. Yeager and Janos, *Yeager*, p. 108.

58. From "Chuck Yeager: Congressional Medal of Honor," www.chuckyeager.com.

For Further Reading

Clarence E. "Bud" Anderson, *To Fly and Fight: Memoirs of a Triple Ace*. Pacifica, CA: Pacifica Military History, 1990. A well-written autobiography by Yeager's best friend. Contains plenty of World War II anecdotes that provide insight into what it was like to be a hotshot fighter pilot back then.

Jeffrey Ethell, ed., *There Once Was a War*. New York: Penguin Books, 1995. Rare color photographs of World War II with commentary by Chuck Yeager and Bud Anderson.

Richard P. Hallion, *Designers and Test Pilots*. Alexandria, VA: Time-Life Books, 1983. A well-illustrated history of aviation focusing on the men who built the planes and the pilots who tested them.

———, *Test Pilots: The Frontiersmen of Flight*. Washington, DC: Smithsonian Institution Press, 1991. A readable account of the role of test pilots in the development of aviation, including a detailed description of Chuck Yeager's first supersonic flight.

R. A. "Bob" Hoover, *Forever Flying*. New York: Pocket Books. 1996. Entertaining recollections of a half-century of flying by a pilot who was one of Yeager's best friends and a fellow participant in the X-1 project.

Dana Marcotte Kilianowski and Mac McKendry, *The Quest for Mach One: A First-Person Account of Breaking the Sound Barrier*. New York: Penguin Studio, 1997. Well-illustrated account of the X-1 project with recollections of four of the participants and commentary by the chief historian at the Air Force Flight Test Center at Edwards Air Force Base.

Louis Rotundo, *Into the Unknown: The X-1 Story*. Washington, DC: Smithsonian Institution Press, 1994. An extremely detailed and technical history of the X-1 program, from initial research in the 1930s to the day that Chuck Yeager first broke the sound barrier.

Chuck Yeager and Charles Leerhsen, *Press On! Further Adventures in the Good Life*. New York: Bantam Books, 1988. The follow-up to Yeager's autobiography, this book focuses on his activities during what has been a very active retirement.

Works Consulted

Books

Al Blackburn, *Aces Wild: The Race for Mach 1*. Wilmington, DE: Scholarly Resources, 1999. Blackburn, a test pilot himself, describes the race between Yeager and George Welch to become the first man to fly faster than sound.

Walter Boyne and Donald S. Lopez, eds., *The Jet Age: Forty Years of Aviation*. Washington, DC: Smithsonian Institution Press, 1979. A collection of essays about the early days of jet aviation, including one by Chuck Yeager on flying the X-1.

A. Scott Crossfield with Clay Blair Jr., *Always Another Dawn: The Story of a Rocket Test Pilot*. New York: World Publishing, 1960. The story of one of Yeager's contemporaries at Edwards Air Force Base. After flying the X-1, Crossfield went on to pilot the X-15.

James Gilbert, *The Great Planes*. New York: Grosset & Dunlap, 1970. Lavishly illustrated look at twenty-six of the most famous airplanes of all time, including the P-51. The text sometimes gets a bit technical for the general reader.

Robert Gruenhagen, *Mustang: The Story of the P-51 Fighter*. New York: Arco Publishing, 1969. A highly technical history of the P-51, organized by the campaigns it was used in.

Myron B. Gubitz, *Rocketship X15: A Bold New Step in Aviation*. New York: Julian Messner, 1960. Background information on the X-15. Includes a summary of the X-1 program.

Richard P. Hallion, *Supersonic Flight: Breaking the Sound Barrier and Beyond*. New York: Macmillan, 1972. While telling the story of the X-1 and the Douglas D-558, Hallion emphasizes the scientific challenges that had to be overcome to break the sound barrier.

William Hess, *Fighting Mustang: The Chronicle of the P-51*. Garden City, NY: Doubleday, 1970. The story of the Mustang and the pilots who flew it.

———, *P-51: Bomber Escort*. New York: Ballantine Books, 1971. A paperback history of the famous fighter plane and its exploits during World War II.

Suzanne Levert, *The Doubleday Book of Famous Americans*. Garden City, NY: Doubleday, 1989. Contains a good capsule biography of Chuck Yeager.

William R. Lundgren, *Across the High Frontier: The Story of a Test Pilot*. New York: William Morrow, 1955. Attempts to re-create how Yeager broke the sound barrier. The book contains much good information, but the author's decision to tell it in the third person makes it read a little strange.

Philip Makanna, *Ghosts: Vintage Aircraft of World War II*. Charlottesville, VA: Thomasson-Grant, 1987. Color photos of World War II aircraft are matched with short but colorful recollections of the men who flew them.

Tom Wolfe, *The Right Stuff,* New York: Farrar, Strauss & Giroux, 1979. This entertaining book about the beginnings of the space program was largely responsible for Chuck Yeager's fame among the postwar generations.

Chuck Yeager, and Bob Cardenas, Bob Hoover, Jack Russell, and James Young, *The Quest for Mach One.* New York: Penguin Studio, p. 135. This excellent account of breaking the sound barrier in the X-1 includes plenty of vintage photographs and firsthand accounts of flying into the unknown by Yeager and four other members of the X-1 team.

Chuck Yeager and Leo Janos, *Yeager: An Autobiography.* New York: Bantam Books, 1985. Brigadier general Yeager recalls the adventures of a lifetime in this 1985 national best-seller. The recollections of friends and family provide further insight into Yeager's character.

Periodicals

Bryan Ethier, "Breaking the Sound Barrier," *American History*, September/October 1997. Story about Yeager's record-breaking flight that appeared on its fiftieth anniversary.

Steve Lopez and Harry Benson, "Mercury's Survivors—and Flyboy Pal Chuck Yeager—Still Have the Right Stuff," *Life,* October 98. Story updates the Yeager legend and compares him to the early astronauts.

Carl von Wodtke and Jon Guttman, "Chuck Yeager in Combat," *Aviation History,* May 1998. From an interview conducted by *Aviation History* on the fiftieth anniversary of the breaking of the sound barrier.

Carl von Wodtke and Jon Guttman, "To the Barrier and Beyond," *Aviation History,* July 1998. This lengthy interview discusses Yeager's career after he became famous and his views on military aviation in general.

Internet Sources

"Chuck Yeager: Congressional Medal of Honor." www.chuckyeager.com.

"Chuck Yeager: Flying the X-1A," 2002. www.chuckyeager.com.

"Yeager Breaks the Barrier One Last Time." www.cnn.com.

Index

Picture Credits

Cover photo: USAF Museum Photo Archives
Associated Press, AP, 44, 60, 79
Associated Press, USAF, 66
© Bettmann/CORBIS, 18, 47, 70, 84, 97
© CORBIS, 43, 51
© George Hall/CORBIS, 87
© Hulton/Archive by Getty Images, 16, 37, 82
© Hulton-Deutsch Collection/CORBIS, 33, 65
© KJ Historical/CORBIS, 20
Library of Congress, 23, 24, 27, 32
© Museum of Flight/CORBIS, 90
© Schenectady Museum; Hall of Electrical History Foundation/
    CORBIS, 72
USAF Museum Photo Archives, 13, 30, 54, 55, 62, 91, 93, 98
© U.S. Department of Defense/Photo Researchers, 76

About the Author

Michael J. Martin lives in Lansing, Iowa, with his wife and two cats. He has written a half-dozen books for young people, including books on skateboarding history, the Emancipation Proclamation, and Chinese emigration to the United States. His most recent book for Lucent was a biography of the Wright brothers. A former editor at *Reminisce* magazine, he has also written magazine articles for numerous publications, including *Boys' Life, American History, Timeline,* and *Wild Outdoor World.*

From the Library of:	
Author:	
Title:	
Date	Issued To: